Mastering Microsoft Forefront UAG 2010 Customization

Discover the secrets to extending and customizing
Microsoft Forefront Unified Access Gateway

Erez Ben-Ari

Rainier Amara

BIRMINGHAM - MUMBAI

Mastering Microsoft Forefront UAG 2010 Customization

First published: February 2012

Production Reference: 1070212

Published by Packt Publishing Ltd.
Livery Place
35 Livery Street
Birmingham B3 2PB, UK.

ISBN 978-1-84968-538-2

www.packtpub.com

Cover Image by David Gimenez (bilbaorocker@yahoo.co.uk)

Credits

Authors

Erez Ben-Ari

Rainier Amara

Reviewers

Ran Dolev

Dennis E. Lee

Richard Hicks

Acquisition Editor

Stephanie Moss

Lead Technical Editor

Shreerang Deshpande

Technical Editor

Manasi Poonthottam

Project Coordinator

Vishal Bodwani

Proofreader

Samantha Lyon

Indexer

Monica Ajmera Mehta

Production Coordinator

Prachali Bhiwandkar

Cover Work

Prachali Bhiwandkar

About the Authors

Erez Ben-Ari is a long-time Technologist and Journalist, and has worked in the Information Technology industry since 1991. During his career, Erez has provided security consulting and analysis services for some of the leading companies and organizations in the world, including Intel, IBM, Amdocs, CA, HP, NDS, Sun Microsystems, Oracle, and many others. His work has gained national fame in Israel and he has been featured in the press regularly. Having joined Microsoft in 2000, Erez has worked for many years in Microsoft's Development Center in Israel, where Microsoft's ISA Server was developed. Being a part of the release of ISA 2000, ISA 2004, and ISA 2006, Erez held several roles, including Operation engineering, Software testing, Web-based software design, and testing automation design. Now living in the United States, Erez still works for Microsoft, currently as a senior support escalation engineer for UAG.

As a journalist, Erez has been writing since 1995, and has written for some of the leading publications in Israel and in the United States. He has been a member of the Israeli National Press Office since 2001, and his personal blogs are read by thousands of visitors per month. Erez has also written, produced, and edited content for TV and Radio, working for Israel's TV Channel 2, Ana-Ney communications, Radio Haifa, and other venues.

Erez is also the author of the hugely successful title *Microsoft Forefront UAG 2010 Administrator's Handbook*, also by Packt Publishing. The administrator's Handbook has received all five-star reviews on Amazon and is considered to be the most comprehensive guide to UAG in existence.

Rainier Amara is a confirmed IT professional with more than 15 years specialist experience in the field of Internet security and remote access. From a young age, Rainier was already renowned for his inquisitive nature and attraction to all things electronic, and by the age of 8 he had already embarked on journey that would feed his passion for IT.

It was in his early teens that he received his first personal computer, but his professional career took off at the age of 18, when he served in the French National Army as a communications engineer. From there Rainier has travelled the world in various roles and has not looked back since.

Rainier now works in the Microsoft EDGE security team as a support escalation engineer, where he is responsible for providing customers and partners with the highest levels of expertise and advisory services on Forefront UAG and DirectAccess.

Outside of work Rainier spends as much time as he can with his wife and three children doing lots of crazy and wonderful things, and when not being a dad he enjoys downhill mountain biking in the French alps.

About the Reviewers

Ran Dolev is a veteran of the network security and SSL VPN industries. Ran has worked with the UAG product for around fourteen years, since the product's inception at the startup company Whale Communications in 1998, where Ran was the first full-time developer of the product. After several years in development, Ran moved to a services position as the EMEA Professional Services Manager for the team. In this role, Ran has designed and delivered numerous IAG and UAG training sessions in North America, Europe, Middle East, Asia, and Australia, to customers, partners, and Microsoft employees. Ran also provided consulting and deployment services for many of Microsoft's enterprise UAG customers.

In January 2011, Ran, together with Erez Ben Ari, co-authored the *Microsoft Forefront UAG 2010 Administrator's Handbook*, also from Packt Publishing.

Nowadays, Ran is as a Senior Program Manager in the UAG Product Team.

Dennis E. Lee is a security, identity, and access management specialist who dedicates his career to helping organizations improve the way their employees work. Starting in New York city at Something Digital as an IT consultant, he saw how technology could help improve people's lives both at work and at home. He then focused on security issues, gaining expertise in networking and becoming a Microsoft MVP in Forefront Security. Dennis is now focusing his energies in the fields of cloud, virtualization, and mobile technologies.

> I'd like to thank my family and friends Doc, Ben, and Rainier for their unconditional support throughout the years.

Richard Hicks is a network security specialist and Microsoft Most Valuable Professional (MVP) in Forefront protection technologies. He has been working with Forefront Threat Management Gateway (TMG) 2010 and its predecessors for more than 14 years, and has been working with Forefront Unified Access Gateway (UAG) 2010 since it was released several years ago. He has designed and deployed edge security and remote access solutions using Microsoft Forefront technologies for small and mid-sized businesses, military, government, and Fortune 500 companies around the world. Richard is the director of sales engineering for security appliance vendor Celestix Networks and oversees a talented team of pre-sales technical support engineers around the world. Richard is currently a Microsoft Certified Information Technology Professional — Enterprise Administrator (MCITP:EA). He is also a contributing author for popular technology websites `ISAserver.org` and `TechRepbulic.com`. You can read his blog at `http://tmgblog.richardhicks.com/`.

I'd like to thank Ben and Rainier for giving me the opportunity to have a small part in this project by serving as the technical reviewer. Certainly there are many who are more qualified than I am for this role, so thanks for choosing me! It has been great reading through the drafts and learning so much along the way. I hope you found my thoughts, ideas, and suggestions helpful.

www.PacktPub.com

Support files, eBooks, discount offers, and more

You might want to visit www.PacktPub.com for support files and downloads related to your book.

Did you know that Packt offers eBook versions of every book published, with PDF and ePub files available? You can upgrade to the eBook version at www.PacktPub.com and as a print book customer, you are entitled to a discount on the eBook copy. Get in touch with us at service@packtpub.com for more details.

At www.PacktPub.com, you can also read a collection of free technical articles, sign up for a range of free newsletters and receive exclusive discounts and offers on Packt books and eBooks.

http://PacktLib.PacktPub.com

Do you need instant solutions to your IT questions? PacktLib is Packt's online digital book library. Here, you can access, read and search across Packt's entire library of books.

Why Subscribe?

- Fully searchable across every book published by Packt
- Copy and paste, print and bookmark content
- On demand and accessible via web browser

Free Access for Packt account holders

If you have an account with Packt at www.PacktPub.com, you can use this to access PacktLib today and view nine entirely free books. Simply use your login credentials for immediate access.

Instant Updates on New Packt Books

Get notified! Find out when new books are published by following @PacktEnterprise on Twitter, or the *Packt Enterprise* Facebook page.

Table of Contents

Preface

In the world of enterprise-class software products, software development companies often find themselves struggling with merely finishing the product and getting it out to the market before their competitors beat them to the punch. In this type of situation, more often than not, the developers are happy if the customer is just able to deploy the product successfully. UAG as well as its predecessors IAG and e-Gap have always been somewhat unique in this aspect by providing extensive customization options which are not only possible, but some of which are even fully supported. Even in Microsoft's impressive selection of software products, there are very few products which offer as extensive customizability as UAG does, and this has made UAG a tremendous success in the remote-access space.

In this book, which is the follow-up to the successful *Microsoft Forefront UAG 2010 Administrator's Handbook*, we will delve deep into the wonderful things you can achieve with UAG customizations. Our journey will explore the many aspects of the product that are customizable, suggest ideas for customizations that could benefit your organization, and offer detailed explanations, as well as code samples for implementing these ideas. Ready?

Why customize?

UAG was designed to provide multiple mechanisms for remote access. It was intended to allow organizations to give such access to any corporate resource, whether it is a simple HTML-based website or a complex, multiplatform dynamic application. As such, it was written with a complicated user interface, and includes a large selection of application publishing templates. However, despite the many years of development that went into it, the number of applications and scenarios that the product can cover can never meet each and every conceivable scenario, and that's why major parts of the server were designed to be openly customizable.

In fact, the flexibility of the customization mechanisms is so good that it allows us to publish technologies that were created many years after the customization framework was designed. The objective of this book is to show you how you can take advantage of this solution and use it to its full potential.

What can you customize?

Virtually every aspect of UAG's operation can be customized to some degree, but generally speaking, the customizable framework is spread across the following core categories:

- Look and feel
- Clients, endpoint detection, and policies
- Application templates
- Authentication to UAG
- Authentication to backend applications
- Application and data flow

Look and feel

Customizing the look and feel refers to anything that has to do with what the user and/or administrator sees. This includes altering the text and graphics displayed by the portal, customizing application icons, changing the layout, setting the server to display additional data to the administrator or the user, and so on.

For example, some companies are perfectly happy with just a simple change from the default blue UAG color scheme, and at a push maybe even apply some subtle text changes plus a company logo, but for others you'll see nothing short of a complete rework, where frontend and portal pages have been entirely customized into stunning works of creativity.

Other look and feel customizations could be geared towards improving the user experience itself, such as by including some basic help or even a portal quick FAQ page, service messages or disclaimers, and of course, extending UAG's language capabilities to beyond those of the default predefined language set.

Needless to say, this makes for a completely tailored experience where the potential here is limited only by your imagination.

Clients, endpoint detection, and policies

The default endpoint policies included in UAG can be tailored to the organization's needs using a GUI-based editor and a script-based editor. However, these are often misunderstood, and we will take the opportunity to elaborate on these here. Additionally, UAG comes with an elaborate detection script that collects over 300 parameters from endpoints, but this too can be extended to collect additional info. This provides the organization with the ability to dictate special requirements, thus providing increased security for endpoint filtering and control.

Additionally, UAG allows you to customize and control which endpoint components are installed on clients, and this provides for a better user experience, as it can reduce the number of browser restarts and client reboots that result in incremental installation of components.

Application templates

While UAG comes with over 30 individual application templates, many organizations find that their specific application requires certain tweaks to the templates to work perfectly. Additionally, one can create custom templates to perform certain automations or tasks, such as manipulation of registry settings on the client. This section of the book will detail the process of creating custom applications, and useful changes one could undertake to make life better.

Authentication to UAG

One of UAG's strengths is authentication and this alone makes it one of the most versatile products available today. Out of the box, it can talk to thousands of applications, and similarly can also integrate with dozens of directory types, from simple LDAP implementations and Radius backends through to the more service-oriented Claims-based architectures. However, enforcing security in the large heterogeneous environment is easier said than done. Quite often you'll find that many of these organizations employ multiple systems or custom authentication schemes (such as elaborate smartcard or certificate-based authentication) to control and restrict access into the multitude of systems and applications dispersed across their estates. In most cases, this can often require a bespoke implementation that has been specifically built around the organization's needs and practices. See the challenge? Then also consider how you provide remote access into these resources. If you haven't already guessed, this is where UAG really comes into its own and the fact that its authentication code is written almost exclusively using ASP means it is able to offer unparalleled flexibility and diversity when faced with such challenges. This section of the book will guide you through some of the things you can accomplish through code customization.

Authentication to backend applications

Most organizations that use UAG use it to publish many applications, and sometimes as many as a few dozen. UAG's ability to perform Single-Sign-On (SSO) to these applications is a key factor in choosing UAG over other solutions. UAG's SSO mechanism is exceptionally clever, and is able to handle standard 401 authentication, Kerberos Constrained Delegation (KCD), Active Directory Federation Services (ADFS), and more. This section of the book will discuss how to adapt UAG to perform custom SSO to applications it was not designed to handle, as well as customizing the authentication flow itself.

Application and data flow

As a reverse proxy, it is UAG's primary job to fetch data from backend servers and present it to clients, as well as receive information from clients and send it back to the backend. Two major components of this engine are the Application Wrapper (also known as AppWrap) and SRA, which have the capacity to alter content on the fly. These components are a critical part of the application publishing process, and can also be used to enhance applications' functionality, while also optimizing the user experience by altering content in real time. By customizing these components, one can achieve better application compatibility, as well as enhanced performance, functionality, and security that go beyond what UAG provides out of the box. This section of the book will guide you in customizing the AppWrap and SRA, and suggests how you can use them to solve problems, boost productivity, and achieve incredible results.

Why is UAG so unique in this realm?

Two things make UAG an exceptional product from a customization point-of-view. First, it includes a mechanism that makes it easy to add, change, or remove custom code with a reduced risk of causing harm to the default core code. This mechanism, commonly known as **CustomUpdate**, allows the customizer to populate specially designated folders with custom files, and UAG's engine automatically detects these files and incorporates them into its code. For example, if you want to have the portal display your own icon when showing **Citrix** applications, all you have to do is create the graphic file, name it appropriately, and place it in the correct folder. UAG will recognize it right away, without you needing to configure any settings or edit any complicated configuration files. Don't like the change? Remove the file, or overwrite it with another, and your changes are applied right away.

Secondly, a significant portion of UAG's code is written using **Active Server Pages (ASP)**, Microsoft's Web application framework. This means that you can open and read some of UAG's code directly off your server, without having to plough through mountains of **API** documentation. This doesn't mean it's a piece of cake—following the hundreds of code files and the interlinking between them can be quite challenging, but almost all of the code is available to anyone, and you don't even have to install expensive development studio suites.

On the other hand, customizing the code is not going to be a walk in the park, we can promise you that. Besides having tons of ASP code to melt your brains, you will find out that the code flow is mostly undocumented, and unless you are a veteran developer yourself, you may find it hard to understand exactly what does what, and where you can add stuff without risking stability. Additionally, big parts of UAG's code go back many years into the past, to the days the first generation of the product was developed. Some parts of the code have been around for many years, and some may be completely irrelevant to the product's operation, but were kept for backwards-compatibility. This may cause some confusion, at least until you get the hang of things. In addition to all of the preceding info, the code, as far as ASP is concerned, includes a mix of **COM objects**, **ActiveX**, **Java**, **HTML**, **CSS,** and **JavaScript** code. For some customizations, you will need to know many or all of them to be able to follow it through. Are you up to the challenge?

What this book covers

Chapter 1, Customization Building Blocks, discusses some of the operations of UAG in depth, and introduces the various technologies used as part of the customization process. It explains some key concepts that are required and lists other topics that will be required to perform such customizations properly. It also includes references to additional recommended reading.

Chapter 2, Customizing UAG's Look and Feel, will teach you how to perform various look and feel customizations, including text, languages, themes, images, JavaScript, and icons.

Chapter 3, Customizing Endpoint Detection and Policies, will guide you through the process of creating custom endpoint detection using VBScript and the UAG COM object model, as well as integrating the detection script with endpoint policies.

Chapter 4, The Application Wrapper and SRA, will explore how to take advantage of the Application Wrapper and SRA, which enable UAG to alter content on-the-fly. The chapter will also suggest how to use this mechanism to improve application compatibility and fix various content-parsing related issues.

Chapter 5, Creating Custom Application Templates, will discuss creating, editing, and customizing the default SSL-VPN templates, as well as creating new ones which can be used to let UAG run special scripts and commands on clients, and applications with special properties.

Chapter 6, Custom Certificate Authentication, will teach you how to create a custom authentication repository that can authenticate a user via a Smartcard or certificate.

Chapter 7, Custom Authentication Repositories, will go through creating custom authentication repositories that can interact with various types of authentication mechanisms that are not available with the built-in repositories.

Chapter 8, Extending the Login Process with Customization, will discuss the process of customizing the login and validation process, including extracting user and session information and manipulating it.

Chapter 9, Customizing Endpoint Components, will teach you how to configure the endpoint client components for customized distribution, making deployment easier.

Chapter 10, Additional Customizations, will discuss various other customizations that do not belong to the other classifications.

What you need for this book

First, you will require a thorough understanding of UAG and its out-of-the-box configuration. You will need to have a good understanding of key concepts in the UAG world, such as the following:

- **Trunks**
- Applications
- Endpoint detection
- **RuleSet**
- Public URLs
- The UAG Portal
- **SSL-VPN**
- Tunneled Applications
- Tracing

All of the preceding concepts can be learned using UAG's online documentation (`http://technet.microsoft.com/en-us/library/ff358694.aspx`), as well as by referring to the book to which this is a follow-up: *Microsoft Forefront UAG 2010 Administrator's Handbook* (`http://www.packtpub.com/microsoft-forefront-uag-2010-administrators-handbook/book`).

In addition, you will require some level of understanding of the following underlying technologies:

- Windows Server
- Windows clients
- Networking (TCP/IP, Windows Networking, **WAN**)
- Active Directory
- The HTTP and HTTPS protocols
- Public Key Infrastructure
- The Kerberos authentication protocol
- Claims-based access control authorization model
- AD FS
- ASP
- COM programming
- ActiveX
- Java
- HTML
- CSS
- JavaScript
- WMI
- VBScript
- Windows Shell scripting (Batch files)
- XML

The preceding list is in no particular order, and being an expert on these is not essential. However, it would be of an advantage as customizations will vary and sometimes require only simple HTML and CSS knowledge, while others may focus on ASP, XML, and VBScript. Equally, a good grasp of networking, Windows Servers, and Windows clients is somewhat important and are all areas that require a good foundation.

This is particularly true when working with protocols, such as HTTP and HTTPS. Most of the others will only require basic understanding. The first chapter will describe these technologies in more detail.

Who this book is for

Since its release, UAG has evolved to be one of the most popular remote access solutions in the market. When compared to its predecessors, it has also become more of a mainstream product which is now widely used across all industries. The appeal to most is, without a doubt, its reputation for doing exactly as it says on the box, but then also having this almost boundless ability to satisfy almost every possible requirement.

In a sense, you could even class UAG as more of a platform for bringing remote users and their applications together in a single place. However, it goes without saying that how you deliver, secure, and then present your solution, is only as good as the person who implements it.

For this reason, most companies choose to either engage a security practice which offers UAG skills or in quite a lot of cases prefer to put their own consultant through training, along with a purchase of our very own *Microsoft Forefront UAG 2010 Administrator's Handbook* as a means of getting up to speed.

Having the right skills is important as many of UAG's advanced features require careful planning and experience with UAG itself. It can also require experience with the underlying technologies and products, such as **Windows Server**, **Active Directory**, the **HTTP** and **HTTPS** Protocols, **Public Key Infrastructure**, the **Kerberos** authentication protocol, the claims-based access control authorization model (used in **AD FS**), and many others. For these reasons, this book will be most useful to such consultants who are interested in advancing their deployment skills to include custom UAG scenarios. This book can also be very useful for network and security engineers who deploy and use the product, and are interested in deploying advanced scenarios without help from a consultant, or who need to expand on the work of a consultant, or to support it following the deployment handover. Another target group are prospective developers who are interested in developing custom solutions or add-ons to UAG, to be used within their organizations, or to be offered to the public.

Conventions

In this book, you will find a number of styles of text that distinguish between different kinds of information. Here are some examples of these styles, and an explanation of their meaning.

Code words in text are shown as follows: "First, we execute the function `GetAuthenticatedUserDetails`, which would return empty if the user has already authenticated."

A block of code is set as follows:

```
<Policies>
  <Policy>
    <Name>Screen Saver Active</Name>
    <ID>Screen_Saver_Running</ID>
    <Type>0</Type>
    <Value>false</Value>
    <Description></Description>
    <Section>Variables\System</Section>
  </Policy>
</Policies>
```

Any command-line input or output is written as follows:

```
@echo If WScript.Arguments.length =0 Then >%temp%\SetDns.vbs
```

New terms and **important words** are shown in bold. Words that you see on the screen, in menus or dialog boxes for example, appear in the text like this: "This option can be changed in the **Web Settings** tab."

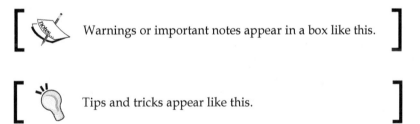

Warnings or important notes appear in a box like this.

Tips and tricks appear like this.

Reader feedback

Feedback from our readers is always welcome. Let us know what you think about this book—what you liked or may have disliked. Reader feedback is important for us to develop titles that you really get the most out of.

To send us general feedback, simply send an e-mail to feedback@packtpub.com, and mention the book title via the subject of your message.

If there is a book that you need and would like to see us publish, please send us a note in the **SUGGEST A TITLE** form on www.packtpub.com or e-mail suggest@packtpub.com.

If there is a topic that you have expertise in and you are interested in either writing or contributing to a book, see our author guide on www.packtpub.com/authors.

Customer support

Now that you are the proud owner of a Packt book, we have a number of things to help you to get the most from your purchase.

Downloading the example code

You can download the example code files for all Packt books you have purchased from your account at http://www.PacktPub.com. If you purchased this book elsewhere, you can visit http://www.PacktPub.com/support and register to have the files e-mailed directly to you.

Errata

Although we have taken every care to ensure the accuracy of our content, mistakes do happen. If you find a mistake in one of our books—maybe a mistake in the text or the code—we would be grateful if you would report this to us. By doing so, you can save other readers from frustration and help us improve subsequent versions of this book. If you find any errata, please report them by visiting http://www.packtpub.com/support, selecting your book, clicking on the **errata submission form** link, and entering the details of your errata. Once your errata are verified, your submission will be accepted and the errata will be uploaded on our website, or added to any list of existing errata, under the Errata section of that title. Any existing errata can be viewed by selecting your title from http://www.packtpub.com/support.

Piracy

Piracy of copyright material on the Internet is an ongoing problem across all media. At Packt, we take the protection of our copyright and licenses very seriously. If you come across any illegal copies of our works, in any form, on the Internet, please provide us with the location address or website name immediately so that we can pursue a remedy.

Please contact us at copyright@packtpub.com with a link to the suspected pirated material.

We appreciate your help in protecting our authors, and our ability to bring you valuable content.

Questions

You can contact us at questions@packtpub.com if you are having a problem with any aspect of the book, and we will do our best to address it.

1
Customization Building Blocks

Before we go into discussing the customizations, we need to explore and understand some basic concepts of customization in general, as well as UAG-specific customization technologies and operability. Throughout this chapter, we will also discuss some of the technologies that UAG relies on, such as HTML, JavaScript, ASP, and ASP.NET, so you can judge if your knowledge of these technologies is sufficient or requires further reading. In this chapter, we will discuss the following topics:

- Introduction to UAG and how it works
- The UAG detection, login, and authentication flow
- Customization and supportability
- The `CustomUpdate` mechanism
- HTML, CSS, JavaScript, ASP, and ASP.NET
- Other web technologies
- Reading, editing, and debugging ASP code
- A word about security
- Further reading

Introduction to UAG and how it works

Ah! Don't worry, we have no intention of boring you with a lesson on reverse proxies—we're sure you've been through that till all your IPs got released. However, you do need to have a clear understanding of UAG and the actual flow of information between various components so you can figure out where best to inject your own stuff.

At the heart of UAG is its main component, the **WhlFilter.DLL**, which is an ISAPI filter and extension. When you install UAG on a Windows Server, it plugs itself into IIS, meaning that every UAG-related request that passes through this IIS server gets handled by our DLL, and that's when the magic happens. The UAG management console acts as the interface between yourself and the complex backend configurations that get applied when you hit the activation button. Once committed, your configurations are what control how the ISAPI filter behaves in terms of processing requests, headers, content, and the overall security characteristics.

Significant parts of the UAG framework are written using ASP, and these include the UAG login, logout and authentication dialogs, the error-handling mechanism, the endpoint detection, the web-monitor, and more. Then we have the management console itself, which is compiled code. Naturally, UAG has many other components to it, which are less visible to the naked eye.

So where does UAG store its settings and configurations? This can really depend on whether this is a standalone server or an array, but in a standalone deployment the core of the main configurations are stored in two key locations:

- In a text-based **EGF** file (stored in `<UAG Path>\common\conf\UAG.egf`)
- As a binary vendor parameter in TMG storage (AD LDS)

Other data that is equally important is also held in various XML files within the UAG folder hierarchy, but UAG can be particularly sensitive about it is the two aforementioned data stores. This arrangement still applies in an array configuration but the difference to note here is that the **Array Management Server (AMS)** will be the one that holds the master configurations for all of the array members. So although each node will have a local copy of the EGF file, they will all rely on the AMS to obtain settings that are common to all members. The configuration stored as part of the array includes custom files that the administrator may create as part of the customization process. Occasionally you might run into certain flags that are stored directly in **INC** or ASP files, such as the **InternalSite site trace** flag, which tells UAG to trace the ASP code (more about that at the end of this chapter).

The UAG detection, login, and authentication flow

When a user types in the URL for a UAG portal, the client computer resolves the URL to an IP address (using DNS or a HOSTS entry, typically, or via his/its defined proxy) and the request is sent to that IP. Then, on the UAG server, TMG receives this client request and cross references this against its firewall policies to ascertain whether the connection should be allowed or denied. If accepted, the request is then sent over to IIS, and in turn to UAG's ISAPI filter for processing.

The ISAPI filter is responsible for an incredible amount of work, some of which can be observed from the output of a UAG trace taken during a client session. What actually goes on during the Client/Server interaction is far too complicated to fully explain here, but at a higher level, a client connects and the filter checks for cookies, essentially looking for one that will identify the user against an existing UAG session. If one is not found then the filter issues a redirect, sending the user to the standard form-based portal login page.

 An exception to this is when the request is coming from rich client applications, such as Outlook, ActiveSync, or the various other Office applications, for which authentication can be performed directly (assuming, of course, that the portal has been configured for this method of publishing).

This login page (part of the InternalSite site) forms a part of the core authentication mechanism used by UAG, and to which all trunks rely on for various aspects of access to the portal, such as the endpoint detection and the authentication flow. Creating a new trunk in UAG also creates a new virtual website within IIS with the same name as the trunk. Why would the portal login page be referred to as *Internal*, even though it's really external? Well that's because historically, when **e-Gap** was created, the solution actually comprised of two distinct physical servers. Back then, instead of TMG, there was the external server and the internal server. The external server would transfer session data to the internal server, using a hardware-based device that interconnected the two devices, while offering the highest level of data isolation for its generation. The architecture here was clearly of a different nature when compared with UAG, but certain key components were already being used, such as IIS. The key differentiator was that you had two separate instances of IIS, one running on each server. The external one didn't do much work, but the internal one, on the other hand, was where the clever stuff really happened. A lot of that code is still with us today; hence the terminology.

So, in the case of a session cookie not being detected, the browser would be redirected to the login page, but beforehand, UAG will run through its install-and-detect phase, in an attempt to determine whether the client already has the UAG **client components** installed. Its failure to detect the components would prompt the user with the option to install them or to continue with limited functionality. However, the existence of the components would simply allow UAG's detection routine to initialize and call upon the default detection script (`\von\internalsite\detection.vbs`), which collects endpoint information and sends it back to UAG using the `results` function (more about detection is discussed in *Chapter 3, Customizing Endpoint Detection and Policies*).

At this point, an unauthenticated session can be seen in UAG's **Web Monitor**, and by now UAG has already associated this connection with a unique session ID, represented as a **GUID.** It's the information that was collected during the detection process that will determine the level of access that the user is granted for any particular session, and the results can be viewed within the **Parameters** tab as illustrated in the following screenshot:

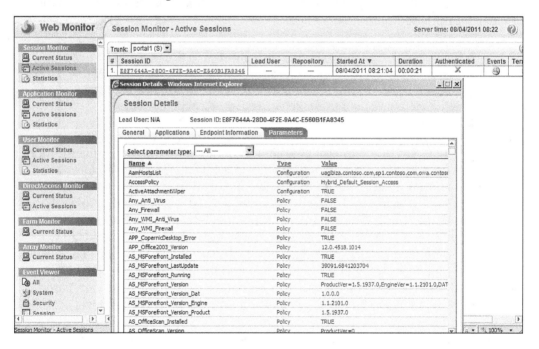

As you can see in the preceding screenshot, the **Lead User** and **Repository** have yet to be populated as the user has not logged in, and this is also represented by **X** in the **Authenticated** column.

It's UAG's advanced policy engine that allows for the creation of extremely granular policies that can be enforced across several different levels. Since UAG trunks have their own individual access policies, we have the ability to evaluate a client's request for access based on what was found during detection. A decision can then be made to permit access according to whether or not a client was able to satisfy a given set of configured security policy requirements. One of the collected parameters is the **user-agent**, which is what a client's browser will send as part of the initial connection process. This string alone is what helps UAG acknowledge the type of endpoint that is connecting, and in turn which of the four core OS policies to apply — Windows, Mac, Linux, or Other (which would typically be a phone of some type, or an iPad). Each of these core policies then also have individual subpolicies that are constructed for a specific operating system, so accurate detection of the type of client is a critical part of this deterministic process.

UAG will evaluate policies using the Boolean logic, so as with the preceding screenshot, you can expect to see a **TRUE** or **FALSE** against many parameters. In general terms, the majority of the results shown on the **Parameters** tab are returned from the default detection script previously mentioned. However, custom policies will also show in this list, and how UAG perceives the returned response can be configured in any number of ways. So, you could expect the results of an endpoint policy evaluation ending concluding with **FALSE** to then redirect a user to the access-denied page.

As part of the login flow, a user will be redirected to the validation page (`/InternalSite/Validate.asp`), which triggers UAG's authentication mechanism. Depending on the authentication configuration set on the trunk (repository type and settings), UAG contacts the authentication target and validates the user. UAG will also collect additional info, like password expiry and group membership. If the repository is of the **Active Directory** type, then directory queries using ports 389, 636, 3268, or 3269 will take place, but the actual method used can also change depending on how this is configured. Using the option of querying the DCs directly will instruct UAG to query two explicitly defined domain controllers, whereas using the **Forest** alternative will enumerate all DCs using Global Catalog services and ports.

Assuming the user's credentials have been accepted, they are then encrypted and stored in UAG's allocated address space, and linked to the authentication repository the user has used, for the duration of that session. If there are applications that have granular authorization settings based on group membership (as opposed to being set to **Allow all users** on the application's **Authorization** tab), then UAG will cross check the user's saved domain group membership info against those set for the application to control access and visibility of the application icon within the portal.

At this point, the endpoint policies now come back into play. As with trunks, each application also has its own policies, and these can be used to control which applications will be available to the user. For example, Macintosh and Linux computers do not have all the required endpoint components to support all applications types, so UAG will detect that and prevent access to certain types (RDG-based applications, for example). After the decision process, the user is then redirected to the original URL he initially typed. If that URL is the UAG's root URL, then the redirect would go to the initial application defined on the trunk. This would usually be the Portal itself, or some other application, if so configured by the administrator.

Fetching pages from applications

Once a user has a valid session, he may stare blankly at the screen for a bit, but at some point, he would typically want to launch some application. When the user clicks on an application on the portal, or clicks on a link within an application that is already launched, his browser creates the request and passes it on to UAG. When the filter receives the request, it analyzes the request host header, cookies, and other header information, before trying to determine to which application the request belongs.

UAG may have applications published using the **portal hostname** method, and others using the **application-specific hostname** such as with SharePoint. Using the host header included in the request, UAG tries to determine if there are application-specific hostname applications that match that host header, or perhaps the host header matches the trunk's public hostname itself. This, however, isn't foolproof, so UAG has other ways of associating a request to an application, such as looking at the **HAT** signature itself (more on that later). Another method is to examine the path of the URL, to try and match that against the paths defined within the various applications. There are additional methods, such as the possibility to decide based on the HAT cookie, if such a cookie was received along with the HTTP request, and the Manual URL Rerouting (MUR) rules, which help UAG decide where to send an otherwise unrecognized request. If none of these have helped and a match is not found, then UAG will redirect the user to an error page.

The following screenshots illustrate the differences between these two common types of applications—one listing a public hostname and the other has certain paths defined for it:

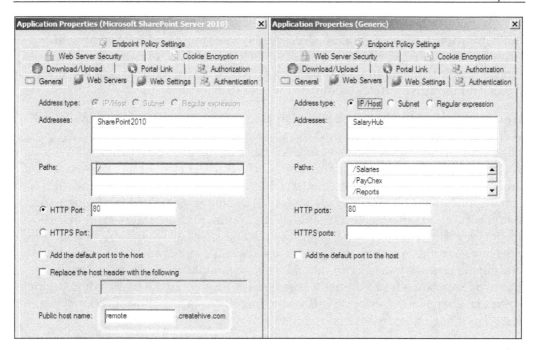

Once UAG has identified the application the request pertains to, it then initiates the same resource request to the real application server, as defined in the **Web Servers** tab of the application configuration. This process may involve some adjustment of the host header used in the request, if the target application dictates it (this is common with SharePoint applications).

The request is sent to the backend server anonymously, and if the backend server is configured to accept anonymous requests, it would send back an HTTP status code of 200 OK, and an HTML page with content. This, however, doesn't always work out.

Single Sign On

If the backend server is configured to require authentication, it will typically respond with something other than the page requested. Most commonly, it would return an HTTP status code of 401, also known as **unauthorized**. This triggers UAG's **SSO** mechanism, and it will fetch the user's credentials from its memory, where they were stored when the user logged in and resend the same request, with the credentials. Usually, the backend server will accept it, and then reply with the content requested. Occasionally, it may not like the credential set, and again reply with a 401. This could happen if the authentication scheme was not set correctly on UAG.

For example, if the backend application server was configured for Kerberos authentication, the application on UAG needs to be configured for that as well (in addition to other Kerberos Constrained Delegation (KCD)-related trust and delegation particulars). In such situations, UAG retries the authentication a few times, and then gives up and redirects the user to an error page.

Another situation is when the backend application is configured for **Forms-Based Authentication** (**FBA**). In this case, the application will deliver back an HTML page with a login form of some sort. UAG has a forms-processing engine, so if a configuration exists for it to identify and work with that form, it will process it and respond with the client's credentials. UAG comes pre-configured to handle some applications' forms out of the box, such as SharePoint, Citrix, and others. An administrator can also create a custom configuration for this, and we will discuss this in *Chapter 8, Extending the Login Process with Customization*. It's UAG's ability to recognize a form's structure that allows it to inject a user's credentials, while also adding the necessary JavaScript into the page to simulate a user clicking on the **Login** button. Some forms do not use a generic or conventional way of doing things, so this is where we can extend UAG's functionality to incorporate additional form data that it may not currently be aware of.

The one key dependency that UAG SSO relies on is that both parties, UAG and the target application server, are configured to mutually agree on a common authentication scheme during the challenge response process. Thus, in most cases, this is somewhat as simple to set up as configuring the appropriate authorization type at both ends, and UAG will do the rest. In some scenarios, things can get a little more challenging. This is where we can really capitalize on UAG's flexibility.

Host Address Translation (HAT)

As mentioned, pairing up a client request to an application is critical to UAG's functionality, and the HAT mechanism is a big part of that process for applications that are not using the application-specific mechanism (like SharePoint or Lync publishing). The way it works is by trying to have requests that come from clients bearing a unique signature that will help UAG identify to which application it belongs. To that end, UAG, when it delivers an HTML page to a client, will parse the entire page contents for links and references, and where possible will try to add a unique signature to each of them. The unique signature itself is an alphanumerical hash of the properties of the backend server it pertains to.

As part of this process, UAG places the HTML page into a special buffer in memory and starts parsing it, looking for various HTML and JavaScript elements in the text. For example, it may identify a link to an image that uses the format `<IMG SRC="angry.gif" ALT="Angry face" />`, and insert the unique signature after SRC, resulting in the tag similar to the following:

```
<IMG SRCc="/uniquesigf872a75338c81cc6d2bc458e795f24b8/uniquesig0/
angry.gif" ALT="Angry face" />
```

 The real signature has been altered to protect the innocent.

After all the changes, the altered HTML is delivered to the client. If all the links and references have been identified and signed, subsequent requests pertaining to this application will all carry the same signature, which in turn allows UAG to easily intercept and handle requests on a per application basis.

Naturally, the process may not always go smoothly. UAG has been designed to handle pretty much every possible HTML tag, as well as common JavaScript structures, but there could always be a miss, and that is something you may need to handle. We will discuss using a custom **SRA** or **Application Wrapper** configuration file for this sort of situation in *Chapter 4, The Application Wrapper and SRA*.

Customization and supportability

As we said before, a significant part of UAG's code is simple text files containing ASP, HTML, JavaScript, and other code. This means that in theory, you can open any of them with a text editor, and change whatever you want. A brave enough person might even attempt to decompile the UAG filter and mess around with that. However, this is not what this book is about, and the intention is not for you to take drastic measures or rewrite the product yourself. While nothing prevents you from changing any file on your own server, UAG was designed with a specific customization framework, which provides a clean mechanism to perform a supported customization.

What this means is that the team who designed the product intended for you to be able to customize certain files, but also that you should not touch any other files (and if that's not clear, most of the ASP pages have a friendly reminder in them too). We will discuss the technical aspects of this in a minute, but the point here is that whatever you do, you should consider the long-term repercussions of changes you make.

The challenge here is that if you change the files that are unsupported for customization, you run the risk of creating a problem with the code, and in that case, Microsoft's support personnel will not be able to decipher your code changes and work around/through them. Even if you are around to explain, they will most likely outright refuse to touch the server. Naturally, if you are a consultant implementing this customization at a customer's site, an issue might creep up weeks or months later, putting your customer in a tight spot.

Another concern is that UAG's own code may change with a future update, overwriting the changes you made or conflicting with them in a way that causes a problem. For example, with the release of SP1 for UAG, one of the default pages changed in a way that caused many servers who had an improper customization to that page to start showing a 500 error upon entry, which basically bricked those servers until the customization was reversed and redone from scratch. If you are an employee, such a situation could be unpleasant, but if you are an external consultant, this may even put you in a legal bind.

In other words, we strongly recommend you plan your work carefully, sticking with supported customizations, and it wouldn't hurt to also develop a detailed test plan. If the task is a contract, it would be also good to include a support plan as well, in case your code needs updating.

The CustomUpdate mechanism

The UAG customization framework is based on a well-known concept often referred to as **CustomUpdate**. The idea is that some folders within the UAG folder tree contain special folders with this name, and in them you can place your own custom code. When the UAG's code runs, it automatically checks these folders for custom files, and processes them accordingly. For example, here's such a function from the page logo.inc:

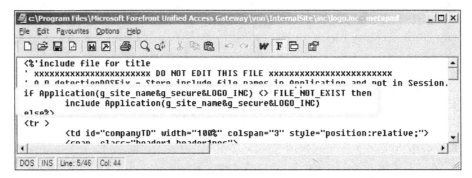

As you can see, the command uses the function `include Application` and defines a filename pattern for when UAG performs its `CustomUpdate` file check. If the file is found, the function will read its content and process it as if it was a part of the original code (the `include` function itself is in `/InternalSite/Inc/include.inc`). The actual filename (`logo.inc`) is populated into `LOGO_INC` as part of the file `/InternalSite/Inc/IncludeFiles.inc`. The following screenshots show these two files:

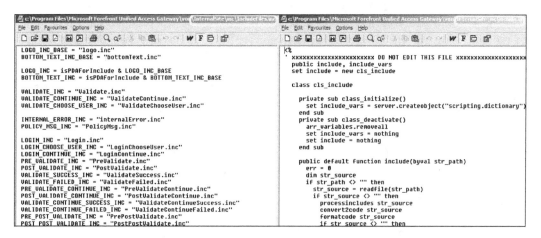

It's important to keep in mind though, that this processing is sometimes a cumulative processing, and sometimes replaceable processing. Depending on the design of the specific component, UAG might use your file instead of the original file (for example, if you customize the **Login** page), or in addition to the original file (such as when customizing the endpoint detection script).

The process of customizing a file is simple: you create your file, drop it in the relevant folder, and name it appropriately. The file naming convention used by UAG is:

```
<trunk Name><Secure><name>.<extension>
```

The trunk name is obvious. The `Secure` flag is either `0` or `1`, depending if the trunk is HTTP or HTTPS. The `name` is the original filename, and the extension needs to match.

For example, let's say you want to create a certificate-authentication configuration. We will discuss this more in *Chapter 6, Custom Certificate Authentication*, but this is also considered to be a customization, as this will almost always require some editing of the ASP code itself to match the organization's certificate scheme. The name of the certificate authentication file is `cert.inc`, so if your trunk is named `Remote`, and the trunk is an HTTPS trunk, the file you will need to put in the target folder needs to be named `remote1cert.inc`.

[Letter case is not important in this naming convention.]

For the most part, that's about it, and the next user who logs in will reap the benefit of the new custom file (or the error it may generate, if you messed it up!). Adding new files does not impact existing sessions, so if you are testing this yourself, you would need to log out and log in again, and we also recommend clearing your browser cache and cookies as well. Some files will require you to perform a configuration activation to take effect, and some take effect immediately. However, it is important to perform an activation regardless, otherwise, the custom file will not be pushed into the TMG storage and may later miraculously disappear from your server.

Another point worth mentioning is that when customizations are done to a UAG array, they should only be applied to the **Array Master Server** (**AMS**). During activation, the custom files will propagate across all array members.

HTML, CSS, JavaScript, ASP, and ASP.NET

So how much do you REALLY need to know? Probably not a lot, if you're lucky. Most visual changes only need basic understanding of HTML, and any modern HTML editor should be able to recognize any existing ASP elements and work around them as you change the layout. A lot of benefits can come from adding JavaScript, such as a script to toggle some text on-and-off if a user clicks on **Help**, or a nice floater to reveal info for your users about how to feed in their domain credentials. ASP, however, is probably the most important thing here.

The ASP web-scripting interface and the VB language it uses are quite old, and a lot of people know them well, so we will not attempt to teach it here. Another key concept is **Server-Side Include** (**SSI**), which is also used a lot. Normally, you wouldn't have to change these, but if you need to add your own files, this can become tricky, because inclusions are very sensitive to folder hierarchy. Some parts of UAG were written using ASP.NET, which means you won't be able to edit them, and even reading the code will be quite limited. Cascading Style Sheets (CSS) is also important, as a lot of the look-and-feel of UAG is controlled this way. At the end of the chapter, we have included a list of books that may be a good start towards brushing up on these technologies.

Other web technologies

A sensitive topic with UAG is the inclusion of other web technologies, such as Java, Silverlight, and Flash. These are all great technologies which can benefit your code in many ways, but they may not be suitable everywhere. For example, including an Adobe Flash or Microsoft Silverlight animation on the UAG login page may be a terrific visual add-on, but one must keep in mind that UAG's parsing engine won't be able to parse the content, so it may be a bad fit for integration with other parts of the code. You may be able to compensate by hardcoding HAT URLs into your code, but that's a pretty bad practice.

Reading, editing, and debugging ASP code

While ASP is not difficult, you may find that the UAG code files may still be a bit challenging to read because every script links to several other files, most of which link to others as well. This means you may often have to hunt through a handful of files to find a certain function and what it does. Some people prefer the use of advanced tools such as Visual Studio, and others are just fine with Notepad, but keep in mind that installing additional software on UAG is not supported. Some stuff is more benign, but be careful not to jeopardize server stability, and if you really feel you MUST install additional stuff, try to at least limit it to non-production servers.

Out of the box, UAG is not set up for easy debugging, but there are a few things you can do to make things work your way. The first step is to enable **verbose** output of ASP errors, which can be done by executing the following command from an elevated command prompt on a UAG server:

```
cscript %systemdrive%\inetpub\adminiscripts\adsutil.vbs set w3svc/
AspScriptErrorSentToBrowser true
```

Downloading the example code

You can download the example code files for all Packt books you have purchased from your account at http://www.PacktPub.com. If you purchased this book elsewhere, you can visit http://www.PacktPub.com/support and register to have the files e-mailed directly to you.

You will then also need to set up the browser on the client to not **Show friendly HTTP error messages**, so make sure that this box is not selected, as shown in the following screenshot:

If you are debugging a production server, keep in mind that the errors may reveal sensitive info to the end user, so be sure to turn the verbosity back off when finished by running the same script with the keyword FALSE.

Naturally, you can add more output to the ASP code with the response.write method and that's probably the easiest way to know what the server is doing and to isolate issues. In cases where the processing is in the background, or too fast to read, you might be able to use a tool such as **HTTPWatch** or **FIDDLER** to record the client-side activity, and then go over the source to find your messages. In case where even this is not suitable or to debug production servers, another tool at your disposal is the **TRACE** functions that are part of UAG's code.

UAG has a code file named trace.inc, which has several functions that integrate with the ASP code to collect data. To use them, all you have to do is add a line of code into your customization using the following format:

```
light_trace "what I gotta say"
```

You will see no visible output, but if you turn on a server trace, the resulting trace will show the text. Naturally, to make it helpful, be sure to put the right data in the trace text. For example:

```
light_trace "Custom PostPostValidate.inc: Entering function 'Read
Lips' at " & now & " for user " & username
```

Once you have implemented such trace instructions, turn on UAG tracing, with InternalSite tracing, and you should see your messages in the decoded trace data.

For more information, see the following blog post:

```
http://blogs.technet.com/b/ben/archive/2011/08/08/enhanced-tracing-
for-asp-debugging.aspx.
```

A word about security

When working with UAG, and especially when customizing it, one must keep in mind that a UAG server will typically sit on the public Internet, listening for incoming HTTP and HTTPS connections. The product has gone through several development cycles, rigorous testing, and deployments, and is considered to be extremely secure out of the box. However, a single line of bad code could jeopardize the entire server, while potentially leaving your gateway open to risk and compromise.

Talking about writing secure code is beyond the scope of this book, of course, but we strongly recommend that even if you are a seasoned web developer, you should go through secure-coding training, or at least a refresher course. In today's marketplace, your company or customers are usually constantly scanned by one of many hackers and hacking groups, and the risks of customer data exposure or public humiliation are enormous. This means not only being careful about what you create, but also thinking about having a third-party analyze your work, or even perform pen-testing on it. We all want to sleep better at night, don't we?

Further reading

We have briefly discussed the technologies used in customizing UAG, and you should strive to understand them to as high a level as possible. The following is a list of recommended books to provide you with a deeper understanding of the topics of ASP, HTML, CSS, JavaScript, Windows Server, Information Security, ISAPI, and COM. None of these are absolutely mandatory, but strongly recommended.

- *Sams Teach Yourself Active Server Pages 3.0 in 21 Days* by *Scott Mitchell and James Atkinson*, ISBN 978-0672318634
- *Head First HTML with CSS & XHTML* by *Eric T Freeman and Elisabeth Freeman*, ISBN 978-0596101978
- *JavaScript: The Definitive Guide by David Flanagan*, ISBN 978-0596101992
- *XML in a Nutshell* by *Elliotte Rusty Harold and W. Scott Means*, ISBN 978-0596007645

- *Windows Server 2008 R2 Unleashed* by *Rand Morimoto, Michael Noel, Omar Droubi, Ross Mistry*, ISBN 978-0672330926

- *Hacking Exposed, Web Applications* by *Joel Scambray*, ISBN 978-0071740647

- *Writing Secure Code* by *Michael Howard* and *David LeBlanc*, ISBN 978-0735617223

- *Essential WinInet: Developing Applications Using the Windows Internet API with RAS, ISAPI, ASP, and COM* by *Aaron Skonnard*, ISBN 978-0201379365

Summary

In this chapter, we briefly discussed some of the basic concepts in the world of UAG customization, and reviewed some of the operational principles behind how UAG works as a reverse proxy. We also discussed some additional technologies that come into play when customizing UAG, and suggested some things you might consider studying up on to make the journey easier. In the next chapter, we will deep-dive into the most popular type of customization—the look and feel.

2
Customizing UAG's Look and Feel

UAG customizations can be very intense and deeply technical, but what everyone wants is for everything to look its best, right? The fact is, a large portion of UAG customers perform at least some adjustments to the appearance, even if it is just changing the title of the portal page. Look and feel customizations are considered to be rather well documented, as opposed to some of the more advanced stuff you will see later on in the book, but the purpose of this chapter is not to repeat that official documentation. We will be guiding you through the actual process, of course, but also suggesting some creative thoughts to get the message across in ways that you may have never thought of. The topics covered ahead include the following:

- Visual customization overview
- Customizing the login and admin pages
- Customizing the portal
- Portal application icons
- Changing texts
- Adding a user-interface language
- Portal selection for clients

Honey, I wouldn't change a thing!

We'll save the flattery for our spouses, and start by examining some key areas of interest that you might want to be able to change on a UAG implementation. Typically, the end user interface is comprised of the following:

- The **Endpoint Components Installation** page
- The **Endpoint Detection** page
- The **Login** page
- The **Portal Frame**
- The **Portal** page
- The **Credentials Management** page
- The **Error** pages

There is also the **Web Monitor**, but it is typically only used by the administrator, so we won't delve into that. The UAG management console itself and the SSL-VPN /SSTP client-component user interface are also visual, but they are compiled code, so there's not much that can be done there.

The elements of these pages that you might want to adjust are the graphics, layout, and text strings. Altering a piece of HTML or editing a GIF in **Photoshop** to make it look different may sound trivial, but there's actually more to it than that, and the supportability of your changes should definitely be questioned on every count. You wouldn't want your changes to disappear upon the next update to UAG, would you? Nor would you want the page to suddenly become all crooked because someone decided that he wants the **RDP** icon to have an animation from the Smurfs.

The UI pages

Anyone familiar with UAG will know of its folder structure and the many files that make up the code and the logic that is applied throughout. For those less acquainted, however, we'll start with the two most important folders you need to know—**InternalSite** and **PortalHomePage**. InternalSite contains pages that are displayed to the user as part of the login and logout process, as well as various error pages. PortalHomePage contains the files that are a part of the portal itself, shown to the user after logging in.

The portal layout comes in three different flavors, depending on the client that is accessing it. The most common one is the **Regular** portal, which happens to be the more polished version of the three, shown to all computers. The second is the **Premium** portal, which is a scaled-down version designed for phones that have advanced graphic capabilities, such as Windows Mobile phones. The third is the **Limited** portal, which is a text-based version of the portal, shown to phones that have limited or no graphic capabilities, such as the Nokia S60 and N95 handsets.

Regardless of the type, the majority of devices connecting to UAG will present a user-agent string in their request and it is this string that determines the type of layout that UAG will use to render its pages and content. UAG takes advantage of this by allowing the administrator to choose between the various formats that are made available, on a per application basis. The results are pretty cool, and being able to cater for most known platforms and form factors provides users with the best possible experience. The following screenshot illustrates an application that is enabled for the **Premium** portal, and how the portal and login pages would look on both a premium device and on a limited device:

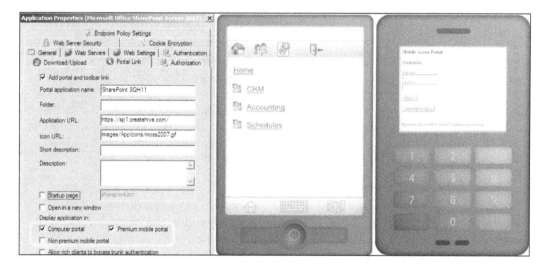

Customizing the login and admin pages

The login and admin pages themselves are simple ASP pages, which contain a lot of code as well as some text and visual elements. The main files in InternalSite that may be of interest to you are the following:

- `Login.asp`
- `LogoffMsg.asp`
- `InstallAndDetect.asp`
- `Validate.asp`
- `PostValidate.asp`
- `InternalError.asp`

In addition, UAG keeps another version of some of the preceding files for ADFS, OTP, and OWA under similarly named folders. This means that if you have enabled the OWA theme on your portal, and you wish to customize it, you should work with the files under the `/InternalSite/OWA` folder. Of course, there are many other files that partake in the flow of each process, but the fact is there is little need to touch either the above or the others, as most of the appearance is controlled by a CSS template and text strings stored elsewhere. Certain requirements may even involve making significant changes to the layout of the pages, and leave you with no other option but to edit core ASP files themselves, but be careful as this introduces risk and as mentioned in the previous chapter, is not technically supported. It's likely that these pages change with future updates to UAG, and that may cause a conflict with the older code that is in your files. The result of mixing old and new code is unpredictable, to say the least.

The general appearance of the various admin pages is controlled by the file `/InternalSite/CSS/template.css`. This file contains about 80 different style elements including some of the 50 or so images displayed in the portal pages, such as the gradient background, the footer, and command buttons to name a few. The images themselves are stored in `/InternalSite/Images`. Both these folders have an OWA folder, which contains the CSS and images for the OWA theme.

When editing the CSS, most of the style names will make sense, but if you are not sure, then why not copy the relevant ASP file and the CSS to your computer, so you can take a closer look with a visual editor, to better understand the structure. If you are doing this be careful not to make any changes that may alter the code in a damaging way, as this is easily done and can waste a lot of valuable time.

A very useful piece of advice for checking tweaked code is to consider the use of Internet Explorer's integrated developer tool. In case you haven't noticed, it's a simple press of *F12* on the keyboard and you'll find everything you need to get debugging. IE 9 and higher versions even pack a nifty trace module that allows you to perform low-level inspection on client-server interaction, without the need for additional third-party tools.

We don't intend to devote this book to CSS, but one useful CSS element to be familiar with is the `display: none;` element, which can be used to hide any element it's put in. For example, if you add this to the `.button` element, it will hide the **Login** button completely. A common task is altering the part of the page where you see the **Application and Network Access Portal** text displayed. The text string itself can be edited using the master language files, which we will discuss shortly. The background of that part of the page, however, is built with the files `headertopl.gif`, `headertopm.gif`, and `headertopr.gif`. The original page design is classic HTML—it places `headertopl` on the left, `headertopr` on the right, and repeats `headertopm` in between to fill the space. If you need to change it, you could simply design a similar layout and put the replacement image files in `/InternalSite/Images/CustomUpdate`. Alternatively, you might choose to customize the logo only by copying the `/InternalSite/Samples/logo.inc` file into the `/InternalSite/Inc/CustomUpdate` folder, as this is where the HTML code that pertains to that area is located.

Another thing that's worth noting is that if you create a custom CSS file, it takes effect immediately and there's no need to do an activation. Well at least for the purposes of testing, anyway. The same applies for image file changes too, but as a general rule you should always remember to activate when finished, as any new configurations or files will need to be pushed into the TMG storage. Arrays are no exception to this rule either and you should know that custom files are only propagated to array members during an activation, so in this scenario, you do need to activate after each change. During development, you may copy the custom files to each member node manually to save time between activations, or better still, simply stop NLB on all array members so that all client traffic is directed to the one you are working on.

An equally important point is that when you test changes to the code, the browser's cache or IIS itself may still retain files from the previous test or config, so if changes you've made do not appear first time around, then start by clearing your browser's cache and even reset IIS, before assuming you messed up the code.

Customizing the portal

As we said earlier, the pages that make up a portal and its various flavors are under the `PortalHomePage` folder. These are all ASP.NET files (`.ASPX`), and the scope for making any alterations here is very limited. However, the appearance is mostly controlled via the file `/InternalSite/PortalHomePage/Standard.Master`, which contains many visual parameters that you can change. For example, the DIV with ID `content` has a section pertaining to the side bar application list. You might customize the `midTopSideBarCell` width setting to make the bar wider or thinner. You can even hide it completely by adding `style="display: none;"` to the `contentLeftSideBarCell` table cell. As always, make sure you copy the master file to `CustomUpdate`, and not touch the original file, and as with the CSS files, any changes you make take effect immediately.

Additional things that you can do with the portal are removing or adding buttons to the portal toolbar. For example, you might add a button to point to a help page that describes your applications, or a procedure to contact your internal technical support in case of a problem with the site. These sort of changes are discussed in the official customization guide on TechNet: `http://technet.microsoft.com/en-us/library/ff607389.aspx`.

Portal application icons

Besides the graphics used by the various ASP pages, another common need is to have custom icons for applications. As you probably know, you can specify the icon name as part of any application's configuration, in the **Portal Link** tab.

However, keep in mind that you need to create four icons, not just one: one file for the primary home-screen icon, a smaller version for the navigation bar, and another set of both for *disabled* applications. The *disabled* icons are used when UAG blocks access to the application, such as when a portal has RemoteApps published and is being accessed from Firefox. You can go ahead and inspect the `/PortalHomePage/Images/AppIcons` folder to see these existing default icons.

The following screenshot shows the setting that defines the application's icon URL, and the four types of icons that are used:

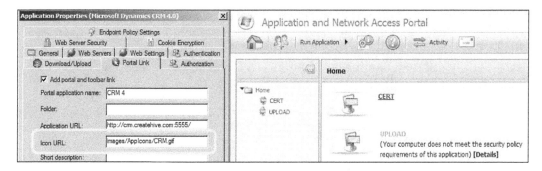

When creating your icons, you can use GIF, JPG or PNG formats, and while you can use any image size, it's best to use the native size, rather than letting the browser stretch the image files on screen.

Stretching images often leads to ugly results, so we recommend that you create the home-screen icons at 88 X 50 pixels, and the **Nav-Bar** icons at 16 X 16 pixels.

While the default home screen's background is white, the Nav-Bar is not, so make sure that your images have a background color that is similar to the Nav-Bar's background, or have a transparent one (JPG files can't do that, but GIF and PNG can).

Even though you specify only one icon filename in the **Icon URL** setting, UAG will automatically look for and use the following naming conventions for the other icons:

- Normal icon: `<file name>.gif`
- Normal disabled icon: `<file name>_dis.gif`
- Nav-Bar icon: `<file name>_icon.gif`
- Nav-Bar disabled icon: `<file name>_icon_dis.gif`

One thing to keep in mind is that if you would like to create a custom icon that pertains to a group of applications (for example, for all of your **Generic web applications**), you don't have to edit the **Icon URL** for all of them — simply create substitute icons using the same names as the default application icon uses, and put them in `/PortalHomePage/Images/AppIcons/CustomUpdate`. This is also suitable for certain applications that do not allow you to specify a custom icon, such as the **Remote Desktop** applications.

One exception to the preceding scenario is when publishing **RemoteApp** applications. UAG only has one generic icon for all RemoteApp applications, but you would typically prefer to have separate icons for each. To do this, you have to use a slightly different naming convention. UAG will automatically recognize any one of the four conventions:

- `<trunk-name>.<UAG-application-name>.<remoteapp-name>.png`

- `<trunk-name>.<remoteapp-name>.png`

- `<UAG-application-name>.<remoteapp-name>.png`

- `<remoteapp-name>.png`

Customizing RemoteApp icons can be slightly more involved and an important step in this process is that you remove and re-add the RemoteApp application each time you change icons, followed by activation. Otherwise, UAG will fail to acknowledge the change and the default icons will remain.

Changing texts

The most popular look-and-feel customization going is customizing the text on the various pages. Almost all organizations need to change the generic **This site is intended for authorized users only** disclaimer with something more specific, and many also want to add custom info or instructions to that page. The various error messages that UAG spits out are also frequently changed too. Again there's nothing to prevent you from editing some of the ASP files directly to change the text shown, but as already mentioned it's a much safer bet to stick to the road and avoid supportability headaches.

The text we see is generated by ASP, but this text is actually called from a central XML file, which makes customizing the various verbiages seen throughout a very easy task. Texts that pertain to the admin pages are stored in `<UAG Path>/Von/InternalSite/Languages/en-US.xml`, and texts that pertain to the portal itself are under `<UAG Path>/Von/PortalHomePage/Data/Languages/en-US.xml`. The folders actually contain other files for other languages, such as German, Spanish, French, and more. When accessed from a system that is configured for another language (in the browser's language settings), UAG detects the settings and applies the appropriate language, if it has the corresponding files for it. If it doesn't, it will default to English, but you can add as many other languages as you like.

Adding a user interface language

Adding languages to the portal pages or in the drop-down list at login is another common requirement in making the look and feel much more personal. To add a language, clone one of the built-in files into the languages `CustomUpdate` folder, and edit the strings in it with Notepad, or any other text editor of your choice. Once done, rename it to reflect the language ID (for example, for Hebrew, you would use `he-IL`). Lastly, copy the file `languages.xml` into `CustomUpdate`, and add the language setting to it as you can see in the following screenshot. As a best practice, we would also suggest you only include lines that include changes to the language-specific file and remove everything else as this duplicates UAG's efforts when language data is being parsed.

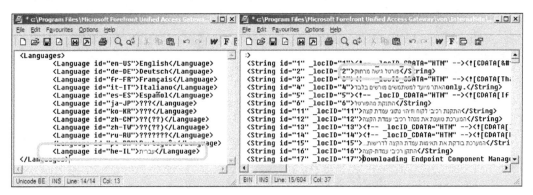

One thing you may notice from the preceding screenshot is the **Character Data (CDATA)** section in some of the strings. CDATA is a special format that is used to insert non-text data into the strings. Since the ASP code pulls the strings directly into an HTML page, this means you can use this format to inject HTML code directly via the language file, and this is fantastic...do you see why?

The reason why this is so cool is because, other than simple HTML tags, you can also inject JavaScript in there. For example, you can add a very long *terms of use* text into a DIV with the style set to hidden (`Style="display:none;"`), and put in a script to unhide it when the user clicks on a button. Another creative idea would be to check the formatting of the username before the user submits the form, to make sure it matches your requirements (`UPN` versus `domain\user`),but you could even save the user's username or repository selection in a cookie, to make the future logins easier. The formatting for CDATA is as follows:

```
<![CDATA[ <any HTML code you desire!> ]]>
```

This is just one of the many examples, but the fact is you would always put security first, and way before usability or aesthetics. Having so much flexibility is great, but we certainly wouldn't recommend using careless techniques to reduce the time and effort it takes a user to login and authenticate.

This same principle can be used for any text string, anywhere. Keep in mind that modern HTML supports things, such as the `position:absolute` style, which allows you to place your elements almost anywhere on screen. For example, you can customize string number `105` as follows:

```
<String id="105" _locID="105">User name:<![CDATA[<p style="posit
ion:absolute;top:215px;left:560px;">Please feed in&nbs
p;your username using the format <B>user@domain</
p>]]></String>
```

The preceding code would result in the text appearing on the right, as shown in the following screenshot:

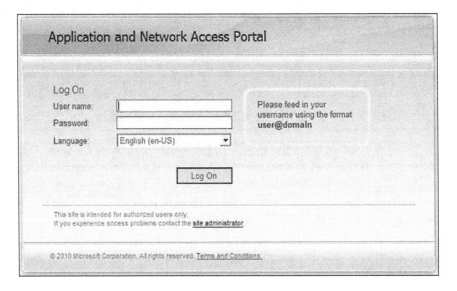

This is not perfect because positioning is measured from the edge of the screen, so people using IE with a different display-resolution or with the IE window floating may see the text floating somewhere else, unless your CSS code is designed to address this. It's also important to check a user's browser and add compatibility code if required. These techniques require advanced knowledge of HTML, CSS, and JavaScript, and are beyond the scope of this book.

Naturally, you don't have to limit yourself to HTML and JavaScript. You can also incorporate animated GIFs, or even Java, Flash, and Silverlight elements in your custom pages. Keep in mind that UAG does not support the latter two, because it cannot parse and **HAT** links in them. However, if they are used for visual effects only, it should be perfectly fine. If properly designed, Java, Flash, and Silverlight can be made to work seamlessly with UAG. For example, you can embed the UAG HAT signatures in links that are inside such files, or use relative URLs with paths that UAG will be able to recognize even without the HAT signature.

One thing to keep in mind is that if you put new files onto UAG to use as part of your customization (such as Silverlight files), the default URL Set may not accept them, and may throw a **You have attempted to access a restricted URL** error. To work that out, simply add the appropriate URL Set rules to the **Advanced Trunk Configuration**.

> Hardcoding signatures into files can be a bad idea, as the HAT signature may change if the backend server properties changes, causing your files to be out of sync with UAG. This should be taken into consideration, to avoid breaking things unexpectedly, and as a result of some network engineer being too independent.

Another tip for text changing

An oft-missed option with UAG is **Prompt users before retrieving information from endpoint**, which is available under the **Endpoint Access Settings** tab in the **Advanced Trunk Configuration** screen. This page shows a notification for the user to allow or disallow the endpoint components to collect information about his/her computer. This option in itself is of less interest to us here, but it is one more page that could be customized if absolutely necessary(`/InternalSite/Inc/Install. inc`). And although we wouldn't encourage changing this file, a good example of its use could be to add a disclaimer, forcing the user to consciously acknowledge the company's terms of use before proceeding into the site.

Portal selection for clients

As we noted earlier, UAG comes with three types of portals. UAG has logic to detect client and browser types based on the user agent string that each browser sends. According to this, UAG decides which portal to send to the user, but it may get it wrong. For example, UAG may not recognize a certain phone or tablet's agent, and direct it to the wrong portal (a mobile portal on a 10-inch tablet would look weird, and a PC portal on a phone would be quite impossible to use). If you run into this sort of situation, you can customize UAG to recognize your devices differently.

Before continuing, please bear in mind that changes in this area do not extend UAG's supportability boundaries, which limits the types of client platforms that are officially supported by Microsoft. Technically speaking, you can access the UAG portal with almost any browser in the world, even **HyperLink** (`http://www.armory. com/~spectre/cwi/hl/`), but the results may be unpredictable, and many application types may not work if connecting from a client that UAG isn't geared up for.

Another thing to keep in mind is that these files are unique in the fact that they don't support UAG's standard **CustomUpdate** scheme, which means you *will* have to edit the *original* files. This also means that when installing updates to UAG, your additions may get overwritten, so be sure to back up your edited files once you have stabilized the server. After an update, you may be able to simply restore your version of the files, but we would recommend you redo the customization (that is, open the *new* files and insert the custom lines into them). This is, of course, because the updated files may contain new and enhanced code that may be integral to its functionality.

To edit the detection, open the files `<UAG Path>\von\PortalHomePage\Web.config` and `<UAG Path>\von\InternalSite\Web.config` (you should modify both), and look for the section `DetectionExpression`. The syntax is pretty self-explanatory — the list contains multiple **Detection Expressions**, which all relate to different client platforms that UAG has awareness of. Then, the four portal types have their own expressions, which refer to the other expressions.

We said earlier that there are three, but there are actually four portals, with the fourth type being **LimitedPC**, which is shown on non-Windows/IE computers.

For example, let's say you want to configure UAG to detect the Samsung Galaxy tablet, and treat it as a phone, rather than a PC. The user-agent string for the galaxy is:

```
Mozilla/5.0 (Linux; U; Android 2.2; en-us; SGH-I987 Build/
FROYO) AppleWebKit/533.1 (KHTML, like Gecko) Version/4.0 Mobile
Safari/533.1
```

There are actually several variations of the Galaxy, so your user agent string may be slightly different than the one listed above.

All you have to do is edit the expression `PremiumMobile` and add a command to accept the Galaxy, based on its model number of SGH-I987, which is listed in the user-agent string. The built-in expression for the premium mobile portal looks for various strings already, such as `iPhone` and `Android`, so just append `OR UserAgent Contains "SGH-I987"` at the end of the expression as shown in the following screenshot:

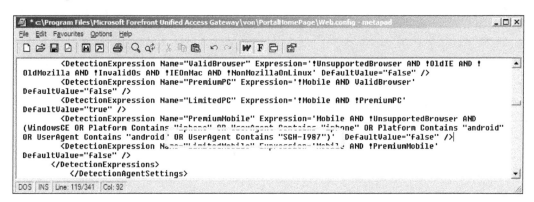

There is more than one way to change or add to UAG's detection mechanism — you can also create a new expression to detect a certain device, and give it an ID. Then change one of the other expressions to accept the new ID. It may not be easy, so the best advice we can give here is to analyze the user agent carefully, as well as the detection expressions, so you can know for sure how exactly UAG arrives at its decision when distinguishing device types.

Summary

In this chapter, we discovered the world of visual customizations, and the various ways they can be applied. We also discussed creative ways to get UAG to look the way you need it to, and explored which are the best ways to achieve it. In the next chapter, we will dive into endpoint detection, and how to customize it to provide the best security for your organization.

3
Customizing Endpoint Detection and Policies

Endpoint detection has always been one of UAG's key differentiators against competing products. The ability to check the parameters and configuration of the endpoint is very powerful, and when done correctly, can provide a high level of protection.

Although the default detection mechanism collects over 300 parameters from the endoint, its true strength lies in its customizability. By writing your own VBScript-based detection routines, you can achieve even more powerful and secure detection. This chapter will discuss these techniques.

How does endpoint detection work?

First and foremost, endpoint detection relies on the endpoint client components. Some companies disable these, not realizing what they are missing, but you haven't, right? The detection process itself is initiated by the ASP page `InstallAndDetect.asp`, which fires up the detection module on the client and sends over the core detection logic (`<UAG Path>\von\InternalSite\Detection.vbs`) via a special JavaScript (`<UAG Path>\von\InternalSite\scripts\detection.js`). The detection VBScript is executed on the client itself, collects the various parameters, and then sends them back to the server as value sets.

As you can see in the following screenshot, this is the function that checks if **Norton 360** (an **Antivirus** product) is installed. It checks this by using the function Whale.FileSystem.Exist, which checks for the existence of a file on the endpoint's hard drive.

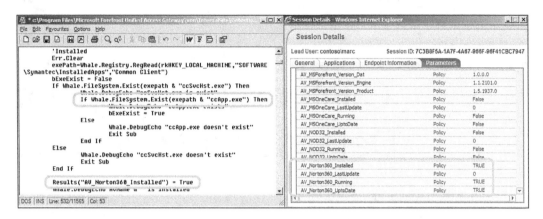

If the file is found, the result value **AV_Norton360_Installed** is set to true, a Boolean value. This is all done before the trunk's login page is called, so by the time the user needs to log in, his endpoint's parameters are already known, and access controls can be enforced. If the trunk's access policy was configured so that the parameters delivered from this endpoint aren't a match, the user will be redirected to the **Access denied** error page instead of the login page. The endpoint policies can be applied to applications as well, though it's important to keep in mind that the endpoint parameters are not re-evaluated — just the policy.

The preceding function is one of hundreds that are run as part of the default detection script, which is over 9,000 lines long. In reality, this function is rarely used anymore, because modern operating systems (Windows XP SP2, Vista, and Windows 7) have a built-in mechanism that already monitors the status of local security software. This mechanism is called **Security Center** in XP and Vista, and **Action Center** in Windows 7. It persistently checks a system's health for various things, such as antivirus, firewall, spyware protection, Windows updates, and more, and populates two particular **WMI (Windows Management Infrastructure)** namespaces with the results. UAG's detection script uses a **COM** object called Whale.SecurityCenter, which can retrieve the Security Center/Action Center status directly from WMI, and the detection results include these, as shown in the following screenshots:

The default detection script is a great source of information, and a fantastic way to observe and learn how UAG detects the various parameters. The object model used is undocumented, so sometimes observation is the only way to learn it. One important note, though, is that the default script is **digitally signed** (you can see the signature in the last few hundred lines of the script) to prevent it from being maliciously changed. This means that you cannot edit the script yourself, and any additional detection has to be done with a custom script.

Things you can do with custom detection scripts

The detection script is just a regular VBScript which can do almost everything a regular VBScript can do, including the regular `If/Then`, `Do/Loop`, `For/Next`, `Subroutines`, `functions`, and so on. It can only do *almost* everything because it still runs in the context of the browser, so this poses some limitations. For security purposes, the browser limits access to some local resources, so you won't be able to use objects, such as `FileSystemObject`. We can't list all the allowed or disallowed objects here, but when in doubt, simply experiment and see for yourself.

The detection script uses the `Whale COM` object, named after the original company that developed e-Gap, a product that preceded UAG by a few generations. This object has multiple methods, and yields an incredible amount of power. The full list of methods and collections is long, so we will focus on the more useful items. You can learn about the other items by reading the default detection script.

- Check the version of the Endpoint Session Cleanup component with the `Whale.AttachmentWiperVersion` method.

- Check the version of the client component detection component with the `Whale.DetectorVersion` method.

- Check the value of the UAG hostname (the URL of the portal) with the `Whale.ExternalHost` method. The method `Whale.ExternalHostname` is similar, but returns the full URL including the protocol as well (HTTP or HTTPS).

- Check a file's modification date with the `Whale.FileSystem.DateLastModified` method.

- Check for the existence of a file on an endpoint drive with the `Whale.FileSystem.Exist` method.

- Check the version of a file on an endpoint drive with the `Whale.FileSystem.ProductVersion` method.

- Check the current running process list for an executable with the `Whale.Processes.Filter` method.

- Read a registry key with the `Whale.Registry.RegRead` method.

- Enumerate objects tracked by the Windows Security Center (Action Center in Windows 7) with the `Whale.SecurityCenter` collection.

- Enable or disable sending debugging information to a client trace using the `Whale.ShowDebugMessages` method.

- Check the version of the SSL-VPN Tunneling component with the `Whale.SSLVPNVersion` method.

- Retrieve environment variables using the `Whale.System.ExpandEnvironmentStr` method.

- Check if a **DLL** is loaded on the client using the `Whale.System.IsModuleLoaded` method.

- Check the local user's access level (guest, user, power user, or administrator) with the `Whale.System.LoggedOnUserPrivileges` method.

- Check the computer's **DNS Suffix** using the `Whale.System.MachineDNSSuffix` method.

- Check the computer's **domain membership** with the `Whale.System.MachineDomain` method

- Check the computer's **Service Pack** level with the `Whale.WindowsServicePackVersion` method.

- Check for Windows components, such as **Terminal Services** with the `Whale.WindowsSoftware` method.

- Check the version of the operating system with the `Whale.WindowsVersion` method.

Some of these methods are pretty straightforward. For example, `Whale.AttachmentWiperVersion` simply returns a text string with the version of the component, such as "**4, 0, 1752, 10025**" (meaning that this endpoint has the version that ships with UAG SP1 Rollup 2).

> The component version number in the preceding paragraph is mentioned in quotes, so as to avoid the confusion that they are four separate output strings.

Other methods are more complicated. For example, `Whale.Processes.Filter` requires a process name, and returns a collection, because a certain process may be running more than once. You would typically check the number of items in the collection and if it is more than 0, conclude that the process *is* running. The following is a code sample:

```
Set colProcessesRunning = Whale.Processes.Filter("explorer.exe")
If colProcessesRunning.Count > 1 then
  Msgbox "Please close all other browser windows"
End if
```

The methods `Whale.WindowsServicePackVersion` and `Whale.WindowsSoftware` are probably the most complicated, because they return a decimal number which means nothing to the naked eye. When the proper Boolean operation is performed on the number, the results can provide us what we need to know. For example:

```
intWinVer = Whale.WindowsVersion
If CBool(intWinVer And wv64BitPlatform) = true then
  Msgbox "The remote access portal has some limitations when used
with your version of Windows"
End if
```

The preceding code uses the predefined constant `wv64BitPlatform` to determine if the OS is 64 bit. There are many additional constants, which you can see in the default detection script, starting at line 8987, as shown in the following screenshot:

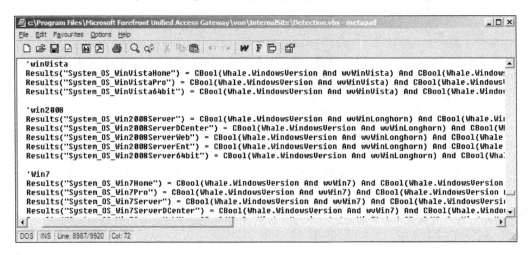

Creating and placing a custom detection script

Like the other customizations, creating a custom detection script requires that you place the script in the `CustomUpdate` folder under `<UAG Path>/Von/InternalSite`. However, there are additional steps to make it work which are explained as follows:

1. Create your custom script file, and place it in `<UAG Path>/Von/InternalSite/CustomUpdate`.

2. Create a new text file, using the following format:

   ```
   <%g_scriptList("/InternalSite/CustomUpdate/<YourDetectionScript.
   vbs>") = true%>
   ```

3. Save the text file in `<UAG Path>\von\InternalSite\inc\CustomUpdate` using the following naming convention:

   ```
   <TrunkName><https:1/http:0>Detect.inc
   ```

This follows the standard naming convention for custom files. If your trunk is named **RemoteAccess**, and it is an HTTPS trunk, the file would be named `RemoteAccess1Detect.inc`.

The configuration takes effect immediately, even if you do not perform configuration activation, but it is recommended to activate. Without activation, the file is not pushed into the TMG Storage, and could disappear down the road. If you are using an array, activation is critical, as it triggers a replication of the file to the other array members.

Custom detection script tips

When writing your own script, you can use any standard VBScript command and syntax, including calling subroutines and functions. Programming best practices, such as properly naming variables and inserting comments are practices that are always recommended. Do keep in mind that you are limited in your ability to use certain COM objects and access certain locations on the client computer, due to security limitations. When creating your own results, do not forget that those will need to be used with UAG's policy editor, so the names cannot contain spaces, and you should avoid special characters as well, except the underscore character. Be sure to study the list of results produced by the default script, so as not to create a conflict in values (or, of course, if you do want to overwrite the default values with yours).

Another thing that is pertinent is that UAG will process both the default detection script and your own, so your script does not need to duplicate anything. Finally, remember that with future UAG updates, the default script may change, so be sure to test your script after each update, and also inspect the default script after the update for changes.

Integrating custom detection with endpoint policies

Naturally, just having a custom script is not going to accomplish anything. It's the endpoint policy integration that's the point of all of this. However, one must understand how endpoint policies work to take full advantage of this. We recommend you read *Chapter 8, Endpoint Policies*, from Packt Publishing's *Microsoft Forefront UAG 2010 Administrator's Handbook*, which discusses endpoint policies, to get the basics of creating and assigning policies.

As we illustrated earlier, the way the detection script sends information to UAG is with the `results` function. Each detection function makes a decision, and runs a command similar to the following:

```
Results("Screen_Saver_Running") = True
```

So, throughout running the entire script, several hundreds of these are run. Some return Boolean values of true or false, and other deliver strings. All of these are collected by UAG for that session, and so the endpoint policy evaluation engine has access to them. This is not enough, though. In addition to creating the results in the detection script, UAG also requires that you define your new value in a custom Policy Template file. UAG comes with a built-in Policy Template file located under \von\conf\PolicyTemplate.xml, and you need to create a custom file (\von\conf \CustomUpdate\PolicyTemplate.xml) with XML data matching the result value or values you want to use. The following is the syntax for such a file:

```
<Policies>
  <Policy>
    <Name>Screen Saver Active</Name>
    <ID>Screen_Saver_Running</ID>
    <Type>0</Type>
    <Value>false</Value>
    <Description></Description>
    <Section>Variables\System</Section>
  </Policy>
</Policies>
```

The important items here are ID and Value. The ID is the name of the results item you are creating, so it needs to match whatever value you create in the detection script, as the ID here matches the Screen_Saver_Running results in the preceding example. The Value item is the default value that needs to match the type of value your script will generate, and referenced to in the policy itself. If the script returns a Boolean true or false result, then the value in the policy template should be set to true or false, as in our example. A numeric could be set to 0, and a textual value could be set to unknown:

```
<Policies>
  <Policy>
    <Name>Computer Name</Name>
    <ID>Computer_Name</ID>
    <Type>0</Type>
    <Value>unknown</Value>
    <Description></Description>
    <Section>Variables\Network\Domains</Section>
  </Policy>
</Policies>
```

If you have a policy that references a value that's incorrectly set in the policy template (for example, your policy is Screen_Saver_Running=true and the policy element's default value is the text Running), UAG will throw out an error during activation, saying **Syntax error in policy expression: source line could not be located.**

When you create an endpoint policy on UAG, the easiest way is to use the GUI-based editor, which allows you to select your items visually. However, if your custom detection script creates your own result values, then the GUI-based editor won't provide you with an option to select them, and you will have to edit the policy manually using the **Create as script** option.

The procedure for this is simple and is as follows:

1. Go into the UAG endpoint policy editor, either from the **Endpoint Policy** page of an application, or from the **Trunk Policy** page of the advanced trunk configuration.

2. Click on **Add Policy**.

3. Give a name to your new policy, and optionally, an explanation (which will be shown to users who fail to meet it, so better make it really easy to read).

4. Click on **Manage Windows Policies**.

5. Click on **Add Policy**, and give your policy a name.

6. Click **Create as script**, and confirm the warning message.

7. In the blank space on the right, clear the contents and type in your custom policy response value(s).

8. Click **OK** and **Close.**

9. If necessary, repeat steps 4 to 8 for Mac and Linux policies. Alternatively, select a predefined policy to assign against each respective platform.

10. Select a policy for the **other** container (which applies to non-PC platforms, such as mobile phones).

11. Click **OK** and **Close.**

12. Configure your applications and/or trunks to use the new policy from the appropriate policy selection drop-down.

 It is possible to add your new policy elements to UAG so they become available in the GUI policy editor. This requires creating a custom `PolicyDefinitions.xml` file, but we will not cover this procedure here. A sample of such an action is given here, if you'd like to explore this on your own:

http://support.microsoft.com/kb/955107

When typing your custom policy, keep in mind that the policy logic is Boolean, and that the entire statement is evaluated to conclude a result of either `true` or `false`. If your policy is only looking for one thing, then it could be really simple, just type the name of your custom results value. If that value is `true`, the policy will evaluate to `true` as well, and allow access to the application or trunk. If your policy needs to handle more parameters, you can use standard Boolean `AND`, `OR`, `NOT`, and parenthesis to achieve your results. Naturally, this can be hard to design even for seasoned programmers, but a good way to experiment without having to do countless activations and logins/logouts is to create a standalone VBS with the same formatting, and run it manually. When doing that, simply create similar variables to the results, and populate them with the values you expect. Then, populate another variable with the policy text, and output that variable with the `MSGBOX` command. For example:

```
'Setting Detected Params
ScreenSaveActive = 1
ScreenSaverIsSecure = 1
ScreenSaveTimeOut = 30
IsCorpMachine = 0

TestResult = (IsCorpMachine =1 or (ScreenSaverActive=1 _
and ScreenSaverIsSecure=1 and ScreenSaverTimeOut>0 and _
ScreenSaverTimeOut<5)

wscript.echo TestResult
```

Can you spot the bug in the preceding expression? If not, writing such a VBS file is exactly what you need!

> Processing of access policies is different than upload and download policies. If this difference is unfamiliar to you, we suggest reading the topic in *Chapter 8, Endpoint Policies*, from Packt Publishing's *Microsoft Forefront UAG 2010 Administrator's Handbook*.

One question regarding custom policies that comes up a lot is how to check if a certain registry value exists, or if it is a string or a number. The method UAG uses to read the registry does not have a way to check this, so to do so, you will need to use VBScript's error handling. UAG's default detection script even has two built-in functions for this (in lines 118 to 156). The concept is based on setting the script process to `On Error Resume Next` so that if the registry key doesn't exist, the script won't error-out. Then, the script performs various operations on the result to analyze it and return a result that we can use.

Troubleshooting and debugging detection scripts

Even though you can test changes you make to the detection script as you develop it even without an activation (except with array configurations, as noted earlier), you do need to close the browser on the client and re-open it to test again. This type of trial-and-error can be frustrating, but there are other things you can do. The easiest way to keep an eye on things during development is by the use of the MSGBOX command to output harvested data. Simply embedding these into your code will allow you to observe the response of each function as you step through the script, plus the information that was collected. For example, consider the following screenshot:

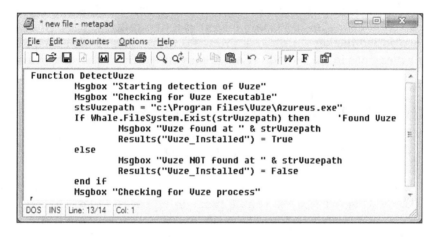

Using so many of those may seem like over-kill, but it's exactly the kind of methodology that will help you isolate those little annoying typos that could take hours to find otherwise. Did you notice the bug above? Line 4 names the variable incorrectly (stsVuzepath instead of strVuzepath), and line 6 would have exposed it.

Naturally, you cannot go into production with the message boxes in place, but when you do remove them and go into production, you may run into issues you didn't anticipate. For example, your detection script may work great on most platforms, but what if users report a problem with a specific platform you didn't test? For this sort of situation, we have **DebugEcho.**

The DebugEcho statement is simple:

```
Whale.DebugEcho "Detection script: Started doing this at " & now
```

This tells the script to send this information into the **client trace**. These are not shown to the client in any way, and to see them, you will need to run a client trace. You will also need to add the following line of code to the script:

```
whale.ShowDebugMessages = true
```

Running a client trace is similar to how we run a server trace. The trace tool is located at `c:\Program Files\Microsoft Forefront UAG\Endpoint Components\3.1.0\`, and you need to launch `trace.hta`. If the person launching the trace is *not* a local administrator, open an administrator command prompt, navigate to the trace folder mentioned just now, and run the file from it.

Once the trace is done, decode it using the TMF files that are publicly available at `http://www.microsoft.com/download/en/details.aspx?displaylang=en&id=15651` and inspect it for your messages. In the preceding example, we added the keyword `Detection Script:`, which makes it easier to locate your messages in the big pile of data that you would find in a typical trace.

Endpoint detection in the real world

The purpose of endpoint detection is to allow us to control access, and ultimately deny computers that don't meet our security policy criteria. If the requirements are simply to check for the existence of antivirus software, or a specific version of Windows, then there's really no need for customization. A custom detection script comes in handy when we want to validate something beyond that. The requirement that comes up most often is the need to verify that the computer is a **corporate asset**, as opposed to some random computer the user happens to be using.

The default endpoint detection allows us to check the computer's **domain**, and match it against the one we specify. However, this is clearly not very secure, as the comparison is textual and anyone can spoof this rather easily.

With a custom detection, you could implement other ways. For example, you could plant a specific file somewhere on the hard drive of every corporate computer, and then use the custom detection to look for it, and validate its properties (file version, date last modified, and so on). You could also inspect another domain-related variable, such as `LogonServer`, or configure the computer with a specific environment variable that's unique to your domain. You could also place a specific program that is unique to your organization on every computer, and check if that process is running as a condition. A little more secure way would be to validate that the domain **SID** in the **registry** of the client (it's used throughout the registry), matches that of the computer object in directory services.

Ultimately, though, one must keep in mind that one of the basic concepts of security is that once a computer is out of your hands, physically it's fair game. A user who is savvy enough can configure a client with virtually any setting that matches a real corporate computer (not to mention other parameters that the default endpoint detection script checks). You can make it harder by checking multiple values, but none can be really hack-proof. An attacker who is clever enough could probably decompile the client components and hack his own version that does whatever he wants.

Is there a real solution? The answer is yes—**certificates**. UAG's **certified endpoints** functionality is the ultimate security mechanism. This entails issuing certificates to users, and configuring UAG to trust the **Certificate Authority (CA)** that issued them. A certificate is much harder to spoof, of course, but do make sure you configure them not to be exportable. Otherwise, a user could export the certificate, and put it on another computer that you never intended to have access.

Summary

In this chapter, we looked at how endpoint detection works, and how you can take advantage of it to provide better security for a corporate environment. We went through the various methods that you can use as part of a custom detection script, and explored some ideas for making it work to your advantage.

In the next chapter, we will learn how to use UAG's Application Wrapper and SRA engine to manipulate content on-the-fly, to make applications behave differently while also solving problems.

4
The Application Wrapper and SRA

One of UAG's key functionalities is its ability to perform on-the-fly manipulation of data that it relays between a client and backend applications servers. So consider this as something along the lines of a big search-and-replace engine. However, what does this mean in practice? Well, technically speaking, this could serve many different purposes and some of those we'll touch on in this chapter, but in general publishing terms, this functionality actually plays a core role in UAG's operation. The bottom line is that if UAG can parse it, then there's a very good chance of changing it. And to put that into context, this is fundamentally what provides the application-specific awareness that is required to make UAG's entire concept possible. Customizing this process can then help extend this further by allowing you to apply your own optimizations and functionality to individual applications, and in some circumstances, even help solve challengingly complex application publishing issues. In this chapter, we will explore the two content manipulation engines that UAG offers, and how you can take advantage of them. The topics covered here are as follows:

- What content alteration can do for you
- The Application Wrapper and SRA configuration files
- How the AppWrap and SRA engines work
- Having your own way
- AppWrap syntax
- More fun with AppWrap
- SRA syntax

What content alteration can do for you

Altering content is critical for the HAT process that we discussed in the *Chapter 1, Customization Building Blocks,* and for a lot of applications, it is equally important to maintain basic functionality alone. For example, when UAG publishes Citrix, altering some of the page content is necessary because Citrix was never designed to be published in this scenario. Without the specific alterations, the user would not even be able to launch the Citrix web page, and instead, the browser would go into an error loop.

In other circumstances, the content alteration makes the user experience more savory. For example, when OWA is published through UAG, the **Sign out** button that OWA usually displays is removed by UAG, with the intention that the user would instead be forced to use the portal frame's **Log Off** button, located on the UAG toolbar as shown in the following screenshot:

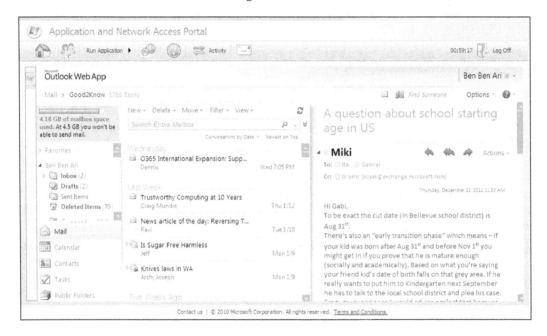

UAG has two mechanisms for manipulating content. One is called **The Application Wrapper** (**AppWrap** for short) and the other is **Secure Remote Access** (**SRA**). As with most customizations, these can both be configured through their respective files, but UAG comes preconfigured out of the box with default alteration code that gets applied automatically in certain circumstances and scenarios.

HAT is probably the best example of this default logic in action, and in this scenario the engines know of all the HTML tags that UAG should look for. With this, it has the ability to intercept HTML elements containing links, so that it can sign the URLs found in the response back to the client. For instance, UAG is configured to look for the IMG HTML tag, which is used to embed images in HTML pages, and inside that tag, look for the SRC attribute, which is where the link to the image file would be. When that link is found, UAG will rewrite it to include the HAT signature.

For example, before HAT is applied the code may look similar to the following line of code:

```
<img src="CreateHiveLogo.gif" alt="CreateHive Logo" />
```

Whereas after HAT is applied, it will look more as shown in the following code:

```
<img src="https://remote.createhive.com/uniquesig932814f7f3e
1197dbf8e3105690523eaedf4b8fa30977329b63b23e65d8cbc8868fb5af9e91
fd3a1c405dc86ecaed7a1/uniquesig0/CreateHiveLogo.gif" alt="
CreateHive Logo" />
```

In addition, the default configuration includes a list of application-specific changes. We already mentioned Citrix, which requires special cookie-handling to work properly when published via UAG. SharePoint is another challenging application, and it too requires some special changes, along with many other types of applications. Quite often, you'll discover that a published application isn't functioning as expected, and sometimes, applying custom configurations of this sort can be the most appropriate solution.

The Application Wrapper and SRA configuration files

The master Application Wrapper configuration file is located at `<UAG Path>\von\conf\WizardDefaults\AppWrapTemplates`, and this folder has two files:

* `HTTP_WhlFiltAppWrap_ForPortal.xml`
* `HTTPS_WhlFiltAppWrap_ForPortal.xml`

When you create and activate a trunk, UAG builds its configuration with the contents of either of these two files, depending on the trunk type, and the resulting file is then placed in the trunk's configuration folder:

```
<UAG Path>\von\conf\websites\<Trunk name>\conf
```

As part of this, the file is then also renamed to be either `WhlFiltAppWrap_HTTP.xml`, or...you guessed it...`WhlFiltAppWrap_HTTPS.xml`.

The master SRA configuration file is located at `<UAG Path>\von\conf\SRATemplates`, and this folder contains two files:

- `WhlFiltSecureRemote_HTTP.xml`
- `WhlFiltSecureRemote_HTTPS.xml`

As with the AppWrap, UAG will again populate a new trunk's configurations with either of these two, depending on the trunk type. Only this time, the per-trunk file retains its original name of `WhlFiltSecureRemote_HTTP.xml` or `WhlFiltSecureRemote_HTTPS.xml`. The propagation process happens during activation, which also means that if you attempt to edit the per-trunk file directly, your changes will be overwritten upon the next activation.

Within those files, you will find many configuration groups pertaining to different applications types. In the following screenshot, you can see a piece of the master AppWrap file on the left, and SRA on the right:

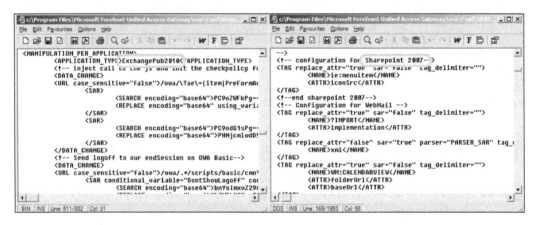

How the AppWrap and SRA engines work

It's a good exercise to explore these files and to understand what they do; not only as a way of learning and getting better acquainted with the formatting, but also as a way of being able to explain behavior that you didn't understand, or were not aware of. For example, at the beginning of the chapter, we mentioned OWA and how UAG removes the default **Sign out** button from it so that the user will use UAG's **Log Off** button. This is achieved with the following function:

This may not make much sense in its current form, because the text is encoded using **Base64**, but in principal you should able to see how this function is used to search for some text, and replace it with another. The thing to watch out for here is that XML files are text-based and some of the special characters used to make up the structure of these files, are also commonly found in HTML and Java. This means that whatever you define inside your tags as values, will be treated literally. So in other words, certain characters are XML control characters and cannot be used as values within tags, as they are then reserved or also known as *illegal characters*. Base64 encoding is used extensively in XML files and mainly to work around the characteristics of the XML structure by converting any text string to one that is represented by alphanumeric characters only. This way, placing a < character inside an element will not cause the XML parser to interpret this as the start of a new element. A non-encoded example would look similar to the following:

```
<SAR>
  <SEARCH><body><SEARCH>
  <REPLACE><body><div id="container"><REPLACE>
</SAR>
```

So as you'll probably agree, it makes complete sense to encode our search and replace strings accordingly:

```
<SAR>
  <SEARCH encoding="base64">PGJvZHk+<SEARCH>
  <REPLACE encoding="base64">PGJvZHk+PGRpdiBpZD2UY29udGFpbmVylD4=<REP
LACE>
</SAR>
```

It's very important that you don't overlook this area as the use of so-called *illegal characters* will have serious implications on the portal's functionality and could cause the portal to stop working until any discrepancies are resolved. Converting the actual content is possible by using any of the many utilities that encode and decode Base64 strings. UAG itself comes with its very own, in the form of a text editor that has **To 64** and **From 64** buttons. You can find it in <UAG Path>\Common\Bin\editor.exe. Another option is to use an online tool, such as http://base64-encoder-online. waraxe.us. The following screenshot shows the same function which is decoded:

We have highlighted the stinger for you. The function instructs UAG to look for the text <div id="divLogOff", which is a part of the page where the **Log Off** button is, and adds the string "style="display:none" to it, making it invisible. The code actually contains two similar functions, one for OWA Basic, and one for OWA Premium, which have slightly different HTML and thus require separate fixes. You might also have noticed the line that says conditional_ variable="UsePortalFrame". This instructs UAG to perform search-and-replace only if the application is displayed within the UAG portal frame. If, on the other hand, the application is opened in a new window, UAG will not hide the **Sign out** button because without the portal frame we still need to log off using OWAs original button.

Having your own way

The point of this chapter, of course, is to have your own way with AppWrap and SRA. This could be handy in several circumstances. One is when the default SRA or AppWrap does something you want it to stop doing. Another is when you want to add functionality, such as changing an application's appearance or fixing some problem with an application. To this end, you can create your own SRA or AppWrap files, and as soon as you put them in the right place, UAG will do the rest to make sure all parsed data is processed and handled by each instruction.

Two versions of the SRA file exist, one for HTTP trunks and the other for HTTPS—
`WhlFiltSecureRemote_HTTP.xml` and `WhlFiltSecureRemote_HTTPS.xml`—
depending on whether the trunk is an HTTP trunk or an HTTPS trunk. This is
the configuration file for SRA and can be located in the `<UAG Path>\von\conf\`
`SRATemplates` folder.

You will need to copy the file(s) into your trunk's custom update folder as follows:

```
<UAG Path>\von\conf\websites\<your trunk>\conf\CustomUpdate
```

This folder may need to be created manually, if it does not already exist but once
done you can go ahead and make your changes.

Then, the configuration files for AppWrap have purpose-specific names and can be
found in the location: `<UAG Path>\von\conf\WizardDefaults\AppWrapTemplates`.

Again, you will need to copy either of these files depending on the trunk type into
the same custom update folder as done previously, and then rename the file to
`WhlFiltAppWrap_HTTP.xml` or `WhlFiltAppWrap_HTTP.xml`, respectively.

```
<UAG Path>\von\conf\websites\<your trunk>\conf\CustomUpdate
```

Do not be tempted to edit these files directly. These files are built from another
source, so they may get overwritten and any changes you make may be lost. The
server won't explode if you edit the default files, but such an edit will be overwritten
on your next configuration-activation. Also, such changes are unsupported.

Keep in mind though, that UAG processes both the default files plus your custom
files, so you need to make sure you don't create a conflict. In some circumstances,
however, you might want to do the opposite, and actually create a conflict. For
example, if you would like to remove the functionality that hides the **Sign out** button
in OWA, you need to create a file to conflict with the default behavior. In such a
situation, the functions in your custom file will take priority over the default ones,
and if you adjust them properly, will do your bidding.

One more thing to keep in mind is that the UAG product team may change the
default files through future updates to the product. This means that after an update,
a conflict with your file might arise, so it's important to examine the default SRA and
AppWrap files after each update. Also, be sure to test all of your own applications,
along with any other customizations, to verify that the functionality you added
hasn't been damaged.

AppWrap syntax

The syntax of the SRA and AppWrap configuration files is based on standard XML formatting, where tags are enclosed in triangular brackets. Each element has an opening and closing tag, and within the tags, there could be configuration information. Some tags have internal syntax that includes additional tag structures.

The most commonly used function in AppWrap is the DATA_CHANGE function, which is typically keyed to a specific application type, a specific URL, and has search and replace strings. If a request for a page matches the URL pattern defined in a function, and that URL matches the application type, UAG will know to perform a search-and-replace on the content of the page. The following screenshot is an example of such a function:

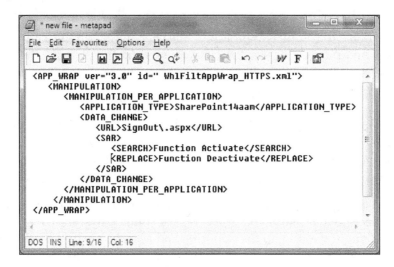

The function is enclosed in the full XML tags of an AppWrap file. You would use this structure when creating your own custom file, but if the file needs to contain multiple functions, you won't need to repeat the entire structure—we will discuss this shortly.

The preceding sample application is of the type SharePoint14AAM, which is the built-in application type for the SharePoint 2010 publishing template. Some application templates have a preconfigured and fixed application type. Others, such as the **Other Web Application**, allow you to type in a custom type. If you typed your own, then you would already know it (and it also appears on the list of applications on the trunk's main configuration page). If you need to know the type for one of the built-in apps, you will need to find the ID manually.

To do this, open the application's properties from the trunk's application list and note the **Applications name**. Now, open the application template configuration file `<UAG Path>\von\Conf\WizardDefaults\WizardDefaultParam.ini` with a text editor of your choice, and use the `FIND` function to locate the application name. Be extra careful when doing this, as any changes to this core file can very easily break UAG's application publishing wizard. When you have found it, look above it for the application type in square brackets:

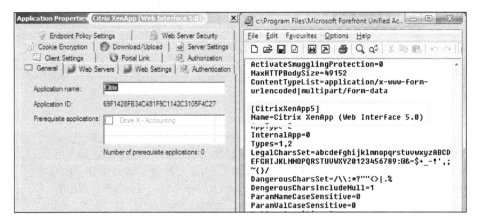

The URL in the example is `SignOut\.aspx`. The backslash is not an error — it is standard RegEx *slashing*, which tells UAG's engine to treat the dot as a literal. If you are not familiar with RegEx, we suggest you review the RegEx Appendix in the Packt Publishing's *Microsoft Forefront UAG 2010 Administrator's Handbook*, or read the following blog post:

`http://blogs.technet.com/b/ben/archive/2011/09/07/ain-t-nuthin-regular-about-regular-expression.aspx.`

When creating your own AppWrap, keep in mind that the URL string that UAG sees includes the URL parameters, as well as the path, so defining the URL can be tricky. You can use various RegEx nonliterals to define a URL pattern that will modify all the URLs you wanted to modify, but you should also strive to specify the URL as accurately as possible. If your pattern is too broad, you may accidentally modify the files you didn't intend to, so be sure to carefully study your application's URL patterns.

A common mistake is trying to take the easy way out by specifying .* as the URL. The problem with this is that it may conflict with finer-grained URL definitions that the default AppWrap file may have, and the cause default functionality to stop working. This is especially hazardous for applications that are highly dependent on AppWrap, such as SharePoint.

The search-and-replace strings shown in the preceding example are in regular text, but as you may remember from earlier in the chapter, we often encode the text within these tags as Base64 so as to avoid XML syntax violations. This example is very simplistic and does not require encoding, but any text that is not strictly alphanumeric should be encoded, unless you are confident that all the characters used won't cause a parser exception. As a precautionary measure, you should always follow up XML file changes by confirming that the file successfully opens in a browser. When text in a search-and-replace string is encoded, an additional attribute needs to be added into the XML tag:

```
<Search encoding="base64">VEVYVA==</Search>
```

Note that the `<replace>` tag may be empty, which will simply remove the text that you specified in the `<search>` tag.

It is very important to remember that the search-and-replace function is a double-edged sword. When applied, this process will perform the replace operation blindly, as long as the string or RegEx pattern configured in the SEARCH tag is matched against the HTTP data. This may inadvertently make changes to another section of the page or even to another page altogether, causing undesired behavior. In certain cases, it may even corrupt data, if the change applies to code that is being sent back to the server (such as SQL update queries). One must plan a change very carefully, and make sure it will be applied only to what is relevant by limiting it to the appropriate application and URL, and if possible, using detailed SEARCH parameters. Extensive testing of the change is also highly recommended, so that you don't find out a week after rollout into production that it causes some other page to mess up.

If you do want to include multiple functions, then the basic rules are as follows:

- A `Manipulation` section can include one or more data change functions
- A `Data Change` function can include one or more URL functions
- A SAR section can include one or more sets of search-and-replace sets

In other words, if you want to perform multiple search and replaces within a single URL, you can just add more `<search>` and `<replace>` sets into the same function, but if you want a separate search and replace for a separate URL, you need to create more than one data change structure inside a `Manipulation` section.

More fun with AppWrap

AppWrap has several other options that are useful. For example, it can do a **Header Change**, which includes editing an existing header, deleting a header, or even adding one. A good example of a header change is to remove or change the value of a cookie to something else, or another is to alter the original value of the referrer header sent by a client. The available options are extensive, so if you want to learn about this in more detail, have a look at the *Advanced User Guide for IAG*. While this was written for IAG, the syntax for UAG is almost identical in most cases. The guide can be found at the following URL:

```
http://download.microsoft.com/download/2/F/9/2F9D9113-B84B-4838-98A0-
A3AEFA6608E2/IAG_AdvancedUserGuide.pdf.
```

Another thing AppWrap can do is change content based on dynamic variables. These are special variables that UAG updates automatically, and when included in the AppWrap code, they are replaced with relevant strings. UAG comes with the following variables:

- `WhlSessionTimeout`
- `WhlLogoffURL`
- `WhlScheduledLogoffTimer`
- `WhlSiteName`
- `WhlSecure`

`WhlSecure`, for example, is populated with `0` or `1`, based on the type of trunk in use (HTTP or HTTPS, respectively). Then we have `WhlLogoffURL`, which gets populated with the URL to UAG's standard **Logoff** page. This is useful because you can use AppWrap to plant that link into a button on the page of your own application. Another example is the `WhlOwnURL` variable, that can be used to add UAG's site prefix, such as `/InternalSite` to sign any potentially missed links. The following is a code sample:

The preceding screenshot is a part of the default AppWrap for OWA, which inserts a call to UAG's cache cleanup JavaScript file.

 `WhlOwnURL`is inserted as is, with no special tags. When the AppWrap is parsed, UAG will do search and replace, and put its own URL before the string `scripts`.

SRA syntax

The SRA engine is very similar to AppWrap, but it does offer a few additional strengths. The primary difference is that SRA is the engine that performs the HAT signing of URLs for every piece of content UAG goes through. It can do regular search and replace just like AppWrap, but its real power is in our ability to teach UAG to recognize and sign HTML code that it wasn't initially designed to.

The need for this sort of situation would arise if some application generates HTML code that UAG cannot recognize, leading to HAT signing failure. There are additional mechanisms that help UAG deal with that, but if all fails, you may need to address this manually. Dealing with missed links can be done by locating the missed links, and adding a custom AppWrap or SRA file that will perform the necessary search and sign of these rogue links A better way would be to configure UAG to correctly recognize the code for the link so that it can sign it automatically, rather than by us having to fix the links one-by-one. So far so good? Then let's look at the following sections that dig a little deeper into how the SRA engine actually works.

The way the SRA engine works is by parsing the code of a page it has to deliver, and looking for various key tags and attributes. For example, when looking at the following code, SRA identifies this as an `input` tag, and is configured to look for the SRC attribute and sign it:

```
<input type="hidden" name="hrweb" src="/formtool/listitems.asp" />
```

However, if the data is formatted in the following way, then SRA will fail because it is not configured to sign the `value` attribute in the `input` tag:

```
<input type="hidden" name="hrweb" value="/formtool/listitems.asp" />
```

This configuration, of what to look for and where, is part of the default SRA configuration file, and you can customize this as well.

The default SRA configuration file includes a list of the various HTML tags (`img`, `iframe`, `frame`, `form`, and so on), with each tag having a list of attributes that SRA is to look for.

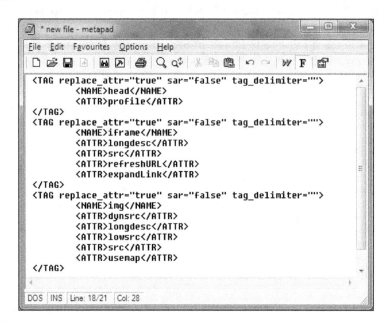

The preceding screenshot is a piece of the default SRA configuration, which addresses the `head`, `iframe`, and `img` tags. You can see the list of attributes that SRA is configured to look for, for each of them. By creating your own custom SRA file, you can use the same formatting to enhance or change the behavior. For example, the `value` attribute of the `input` tag we mentioned previously is actually covered in the default SRA configuration, but as shown in the following screenshot:

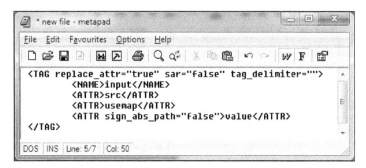

As you can see, the `value` attribute is listed, but the `sign_abs_path` option tells UAG not to sign **absolute paths**. If the URL was a full URL (such as `http://www.createhive.com`), then UAG would sign it; if our path is relative, UAG ignores it. By creating a custom file with this option removed, we can set UAG to sign URLs in `value` attributes whether they are relative or absolute. Naturally, we still need to have the custom SRA file fully formatted, which would be as shown in the following screenshot:

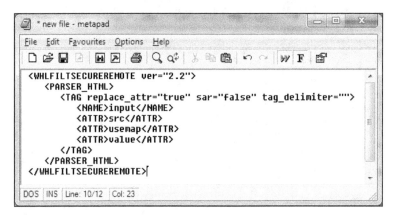

Using the same format, you can also introduce completely new tags or attributes that UAG is not aware of.

However, remember to always start by checking if UAG already has definitions for them, to make sure you do not create a conflict. If this is a new tag, things are simple, but if these are new or different attributes of an existing tag, you need to clone the existing tag configuration from the default file, and add or edit those. For example, let's say that your application has a link as follows:

```
<iframe src="A.html" name="window" align=center action="/save.
aspx">FrameMain</iframe>
```

By default, the `iFrame` tag is configured for the attributes `longdesc`, `src`, `refreshURL`, and `expandLink`, but not for the `Action` attribute. To add it, clone the SRA section that deals with `iFrame`, and add the new attribute to the others.

Another thing that is important to know is that the SRA has multiple parsers. The default SRA talks mostly about the HTML parser, but also about parsers for CSS, JavaScript, and VBScript. There is even a `<PARSER_EXCEPTION>` configuration, which allows you to configure attributes that should be skipped altogether. The need for separate parsers comes from the fact that the structure of code with each is somewhat different. For example, HTML structure uses triangular brackets, while JavaScript uses curly brackets for most things.

For JavaScript, specifically, there is also a list of EVENT_HANDLERS which define JavaScript commands that UAG should examine for URLs. For example, some apps use the OnClick JavaScript method to define an action for a button or link, instead of the regular HREF. The SRA has a special configuration for this action, and others, which you might also need to modify or expand to correct links that are missed in JavaScript code. Here is an example for both options with SRA:

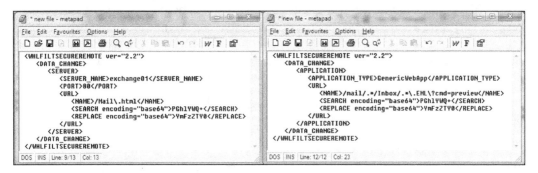

As with AppWrap, URLs can be specified with RegEx, and search-and-replace strings should be encoded with Base64, if containing characters that jeopardize XML formatting.

Summary

The things you can do with AppWrap and SRA are incredible. With clever enough search and replace, almost anything could be achieved, from the simple changing of the background color of an application, to introduce full scripts that can enhance an application's functionality. One customer, for example, wrote an AppWrap that inserts a clever red-acting JavaScript to their e-mail application. Another added a functionality to block access to certain file types in SharePoint by having a script-disable links to these documents on-the-fly. The possibilities are endless. In this chapter, we covered the most useful functionality of both SRA and AppWrap, but there are additional things they can do. The following links can provide you with more information:

http://technet.microsoft.com/en-us/library/ff607339.aspx.

http://technet.microsoft.com/en-us/library/ff607388.aspx.

In addition to this, the original *IAG Advanced User Guide* has about 50 pages of text describing the various functions, so it makes for an interesting read and a good reference to keep around. The file can be downloaded from the following URL:

```
http://download.microsoft.com/download/2/F/9/2F9D9113-B84B-4838-98A0-
A3AEFA6608E2/IAG_AdvancedUserGuide.pdf.
```

In this PDF, pages 289 to 313 and pages 219 to 254 describe AppWrap and SRA, respectively, and are a full reference of all available commands and structures that AppWrap and SRA support, including those that are more esoteric and rare. Even though it was written for IAG (UAG's predecessor), most of the content applies to UAG, with the exception of some minor changes described here:

```
http://blogs.technet.com/b/edgeaccessblog/archive/2009/11/17/
appwrap-in-uag-what-s-new.aspx.
```

In the next chapter, we will learn how the UAG's application templates are built, and how to create custom ones for our own needs.

5
Creating Custom Application Templates

While UAG comes prepopulated with a wide selection of application templates, you might find yourself yearning for something that is a little different. Perhaps you don't like the prompt that says **Ready to launch application**, which shows up when you launch an SSL-VPN application, or perhaps you would like your application to perform certain functions when launched. This and much more is possible by customizing the default application templates, and even adding your own. In this chapter, we will learn the following:

- Building SSL-VPN templates
- Creating your own templates
- Template customizations and enhancements
- More parameters used in the template
- SSL-VPN-specific settings and configuration
- Tying in to the SSL-VPN template list

Building SSL-VPN templates

The SSL-VPN application templates are stored in two master files on the UAG server. The first file is `<UAG Path>\von\conf\wizarddefaults\WizardDefaultParam. Ini`, and the second is `<UAG Path>\von\conf\SSLVPNTemplates.xml`. Collectively, both these files provide the necessary data and application-specific information that allows UAG to build and publish resources to a trunk. The `WizardDefaultParam` file contains a list of predefined application templates (not just SSL-VPN ones), and their associated parameter definitions.

The following screenshots are just two extracts from this file:

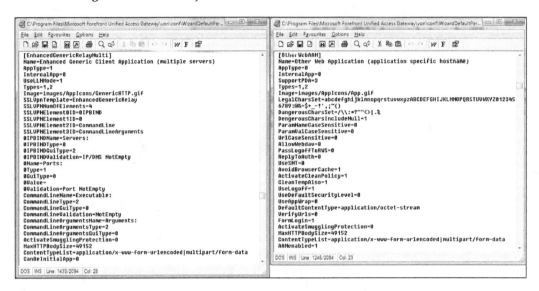

As you can see, each application has somewhat different parameters, some of which are rather self-explanatory. For example, the `MaxHTTPBodySize` and `ActivateSmugglingProtection` parameters will appear on the **Web Server Security** tab of the application properties window, while the `Image` parameter is populated in the **Portal Link** tab. On a UAG server running SP1 Update 1, you will find a total of 55 applications in the default wizard file, but by customizing this file, you can easily add more. We will discuss this shortly.

Some of the templates in the default Wizard Parameter file (`WizardDefaultParam`) are for *regular* applications, such as Exchange and SharePoint, but within this file also exists an area of special importance: the SSL-VPN templates. Any template can be customized, but it is these SSL-VPN templates and their features that are of particular interest to us, as they are what provide us with some of UAG's unique advantages.

The great qualities of SSL-VPN have been discussed in detail elsewhere, but to put it briefly, the big advantage is that it provides a connection directly into the corporate network. This way, any client-side application can communicate with its server directly, no matter what TCP/IP port is in use, and there is no dependency on the UAG filter's ability to understand the content. Essentially, virtually any application can be published this way, with only a few exceptions, and in some cases this can be the only option.

An important difference between SSL-VPN tunneled applications and full SSL-VPN tunneling, as offered by SSTP or classic SSL-VPN Tunneling(also known as The Network Connector) is that SSL-VPN tunneled applications are limited to tunneling applications that use TCP/IP, while full SSL-VPN tunneling also supports applications that use the UDP protocol.

On top of that, the thing that makes these application templates even cooler is the fact that they have a built-in ability to run custom code on the client computer. The following screenshot is an example:

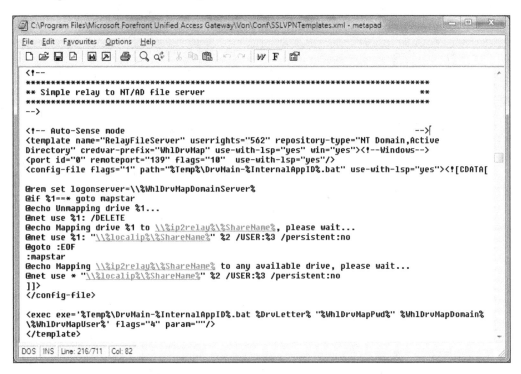

The preceding screenshot shows a template contained within the second of our master files discussed earlier, the SSLVpnTemplates.xml, and used for the **Drive Mapping** application. As you can see, it has a number of parameters, followed by a series of **DOS-Shell** commands, encapsulated within a CDATA structure. These actually get saved into a temporary batch file on the client (defined in the config-file tag), and executed according to the parameters defined in the exec tag that comes a bit later. Doesn't that already entice your imagination? How awesome!!!

Creating your own templates

Like any customization process with UAG, creating your own templates requires creating your own file and placing it in the CustomUpdate folder of the relevant folder. The following are the steps that you need to take:

1. If the UAG configuration console is open, close it.

2. Create your own SSL-VPN template, based on the same structure of the SSLVPNTemplates.xml file. The file needs to start with <config><templates version="3" use-lsp="1">, and end with </templates></config>, and in between, you can have one or more templates that start and end with the template tags (<template name="... and </template>). Consider the following screenshot, for example:

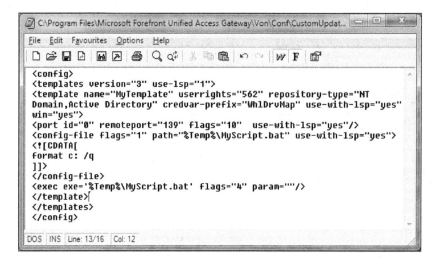

3. Place your file in the folder <UAG Path>\von\conf\CustomUpdate and make sure you name it SSLVPNTemplates.xml.

4. Create a custom WizardDefaultParams file, based on the structure of WizardDefaultParams.ini. The file needs to start with the application list tag, which lists the number of custom applications you are defining, and their names. Then, it has to have a section for each custom app, which includes the application's name, as well as a reference to the SSL-VPN template that you have defined in step 2 (**MyTemplate** in our example). Your file would look approximately as shown in the following screenshot:

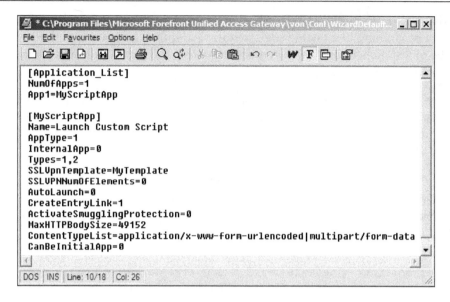

5. Save the file in `<UAG Path>\von\conf\wizarddefaults\CustomUpdate` and make sure you name it `WizardDefaultParam.Ini`.

6. Reopening the UAG console should be enough to see your custom changes take place by seeing your new application template or templates at the bottom of the list under `Client/Server and legacy applications`, with the name you have defined (**Launch Custom Script**).

Before you start laying down your evil plans, though, let us examine the structure some more.

Template customizations and enhancements

As noted previously, the ability to create your own script is what makes creating custom templates so powerful. The **Drive Mapping** application uses this ability to run a NET USE command, which maps a network drive over a TCP/IP tunnel using the RPC/SMB protocols. You can create a similar template that runs any command you want. In fact, you may want to use this to simply manipulate some of the client's configurations without even needing the tunnel at all.

Essentially, you can put any **CMD-Shell** commands within the CDATA section. They will be running in a visible shell window, so it may be good practice to use the `echo off` statement and the `@` symbol to conceal the commands and their outputs from the end user.

What if you want to do something even more powerful? The SSL-VPN tunnel can also run a `.VBS` file, although that involves a slightly trickier approach. The engine cannot run a VBS file directly, but you can use the CMD-Shell `echo` command to generate the file dynamically and execute it as follows:

```
@echo Dim aDNS(1) >%temp%\SetDns.vbs

@echo aDNS(0) = "4.2.2.2" >>%temp%\SetDns.vbs

@echo aDNS(1) = "4.2.2.1" >>%temp%\SetDns.vbs

@echo set objWMIService = GetObject("winmgmts:\\.\root\cimv2") >>%temp%\
SetDns.vbs

@echo Set colItems = objWMIService.ExecQuery("Select * From Win32_
NetworkAdapterConfiguration Where IPEnabled = 1") >>%temp%\SetDns.vbs

@echo For Each objItem in colItems >>%temp%\SetDns.vbs

@echo errDNS = objItem.SetDNSServerSearchOrder() >>%temp%\SetDns.vbs

@echo wscript.sleep 500 >>%temp%\SetDns.vbs

@echo errDNS = objItem.SetDNSServerSearchOrder(aDNS) >>%temp%\SetDns.vbs

@echo next >>%temp%\SetDns.vbs

@cscript %temp%\SetDns.vbs
```

The preceding script uses the `echo` command with the `>` and `>>` symbols to create the file `SetDns.vbs` in the system's **temporary folder** (`%temp%`), and finally, to launch that file with the VBScript scripting host **CSCRIPT**. Each `echo` command is preceded with a `@` symbol so that it does not show up on screen.

In case you are wondering, the `>` symbol tells the CMD-Shell to send the output of the preceding command into a text file, and the `>>` symbol does the same, but appends the text to an existing file. This is why the preceding first line uses `>`, and the other lines use `>>`. Another limitation that the CMD-Shell interpreter imposes on us is the use of the `"` symbol, which cannot be used easily, so we have substituted it with the `chr(34)` command. Naturally, if you plan on using the preceding script, be sure to download it from the Packt website, as the line breaks that the book format imposes may cause the script to fail.

The purpose of the preceding script is to alter the settings for the DNS server configuration on the client to use the public servers residing at 4.2.2.2 and 4.2.2.1. This may be useful in cases where a user's ISP is manipulating the functionality of their own DNS servers. This is done by some ISPs, and could cause various issues with SSL-VPN based application tunneling. One challenge with this is that the modern operating systems, such as Windows Vista and Windows 7 restrict our ability to change the deep-level system settings such as this. If you attempt to use the preceding script on such a system, it will fail. The solution is to use another function that invokes the **User Access Controls (UAC)** dialog, offering the user the choice of approving or denying the operation. The following is the structure:

```
@echo If WScript.Arguments.length =0 Then >%temp%\SetDns.vbs

@echo  Set objShell = CreateObject("Shell.Application") >>%temp%\SetDns.vbs

@echo  objShell.ShellExecute "wscript.exe", Chr(34) + WScript.ScriptFullName + Chr(34) + " uac", "", "runas", 1 >>%temp%\SetDns.vbs

@echo Else >>%temp%\SetDns.vbs

.....Do whatever we want....

@echo End If >>%temp%\SetDns.vbs
```

To use this, all you have to do is place the actual script echoing commands, such as the ones we saw earlier, between the preceding else and end if lines. Naturally, this structure is not required for everything—just for actions that would be considered a security threat, and limited by UAC. For more details about UAC and what it limits, refer to the following URL:

http://technet.microsoft.com/en-us/library/cc731416(WS.10).aspx.

More parameters used in the template

As we saw earlier, the templates also contain many parameters, and you can use these to do additional things. The WizardDefaultParams file contains over 50 templates, but only some of them (about half) are SSL-VPN based and depend on a template in the SSLVPNTemplates file. Let's review the structure of these files in more detail.

WizardDefault

In terms of publishing, the WizardDefaultParams.ini file is UAG's starting point, and this file's contents are split into two key sections: the application templates' list, followed by application definitions.

The [Application_List] is an enumeration of all of the applications that exist in UAG, listed by number and name in the format App<x>=<name>. The second line in this section also has the parameter NumOfApps, which basically specifies the total number of listed templates that UAG should account for. The following is a list of the default applications on a UAG server:

All items found on this list then have a corresponding definition set that is located in the second section of this file. It is this data that defines an application's specifics when publishing. The definitions themselves are split into individual application blocks which are easily referenced by their respective name in brackets, [].

Any duplicate names found will cause UAG to display the application as many times as it is referenced in the [Application_List], regardless of whether it has an associated set of definitions or not. Duplicate definition sets, on the other hand, are not supported, and will generate a UAG initialization error when you attempt to add a new application. The following is a section of one of the default application templates used to publish Lync:

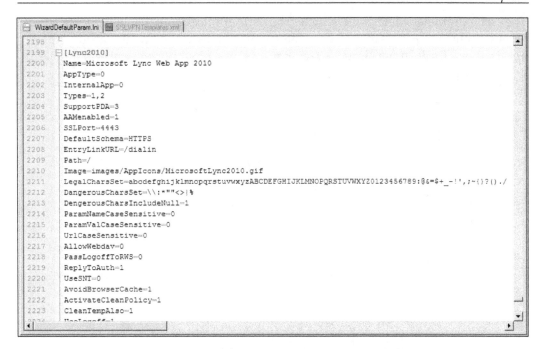

```
2198    [
2199    ⊟[Lync2010]
2200      Name=Microsoft Lync Web App 2010
2201      AppType=0
2202      InternalApp=0
2203      Types=1,2
2204      SupportPDA=3
2205      AAMenabled=1
2206      SSLPort=4443
2207      DefaultSchema=HTTPS
2208      EntryLinkURL=/dialin
2209      Path=/
2210      Image=images/AppIcons/MicrosoftLync2010.gif
2211      LegalCharsSet=abcdefghijklmnopqrstuvwxyzABCDEFGHIJKLMNOPQRSTUVWXYZ0123456789:@&=$+_-!',;~{}?()./
2212      DangerousCharsSet=\\:*""<>|%
2213      DengerousCharsIncludeNull=1
2214      ParamNameCaseSensitive=0
2215      ParamValCaseSensitive=0
2216      UrlCaseSensitive=0
2217      AllowWebdav=0
2218      PassLogoffToRWS=0
2219      ReplyToAuth=1
2220      UseSNT=0
2221      AvoidBrowserCache=1
2222      ActivateCleanPolicy=1
2223      CleanTempAlso=1
2224      UseLogoff=1
```

The first parameter of each application template is its name, encapsulated by square brackets, followed by the display name formatted as `Name=<display name>`.

It should be noted that the application name used in both sections should match exactly as they are case sensitive, and if this is overlooked, will prevent your custom app from being picked up.

The next parameters determine which group the application belongs to. If `AppType` is set to 0 and `InternalApp` to 1 or 2, the app will show up in the first group of applications (**Built In Services**). If `InternalApp` is set to 0 however, it will appear in the **Web** group.

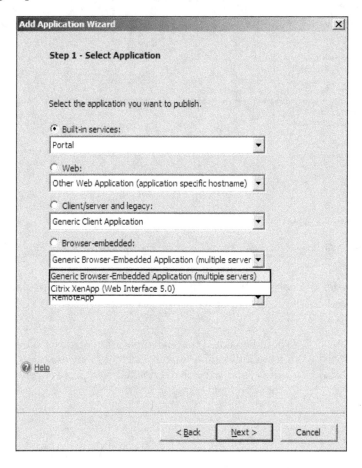

If the `AppType` is 1, this indicates an SSL-VPN app, which will appear in the **Client/Server and Legacy** application groups. An `AppType` of 2 puts it in the third group — **Browser Embedded Applications**. This arrangement changes somewhat for the RDS applications, and in this case UAG will look at the application's name to determine its placement. An application whose name begins with `MSTC_` will automatically be put into the **Terminal Services (TS)/Remote Desktop Services (RDS)** category.

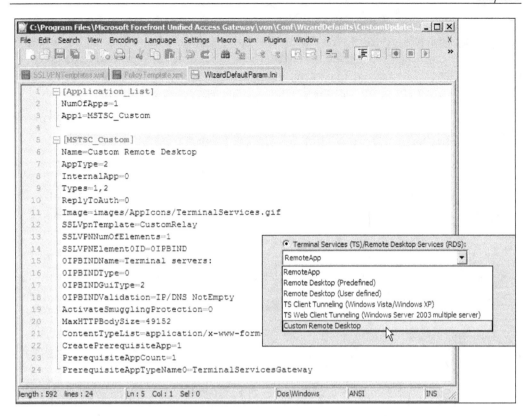

The next group of parameters controls the application name and parameters:

- `LegalCharsSet`
- `DangerousCharsSet`
- `DangerousCharsIncludeNull`
- `ParamNameCaseSensitive`
- `ParamValCaseSensitive`
- `UrlCaseSensitive`

This is pretty much self-explanatory. The parameter `AllowWebdav` will allow the application to use the **WebDav** methods, which are relevant for Exchange, Forefront Identity Manager (FIM), and SharePoint. The `PassLogoffToRWS` parameter controls whether UAG sends a logoff to the backend server, which is relevant if the backend server has a session management mechanism, such as Exchange.

The parameter `ReplyToAuth` sets the template default for performing **Single Sign On (SSO)**, which is a part of step 7 of the add application wizard (naturally, when using the add application wizard to create the application, one can still choose another setting). The `FormLogin` parameter indicates whether UAG will attempt to perform automatic form login if the backend server replies with one.

Some application templates have the settings for **Download URLs**, **Upload URLs**, and **Ignored URLs**:

When these are set, UAG will configure the appropriate parameters in the **Advanced Trunk Configuration**. These parameters, in case you don't remember, define patterns that indicate a special URL. For example, the preceding screenshot is from the Outlook Web Access 2010 template, and allows UAG to recognize when the user downloads or uploads an e-mail attachment. This allows UAG to block these URLs based on the defined endpoint policy. `IgnoreURLs` are used to detect *background* traffic which some applications generate, so UAG can know to ignore it for the idle-timeout calculations.

More useful parameters include:

- `Path`: This setting specifies the default paths for the application, which can be edited as part of the **Web Servers** configuration step. Multiple paths are separated by a pipe (|).

- `ManualURL`: This is a group of settings that add manual URL replacement. This is done as part of the SharePoint 2003 apps, and some Exchange apps as well.

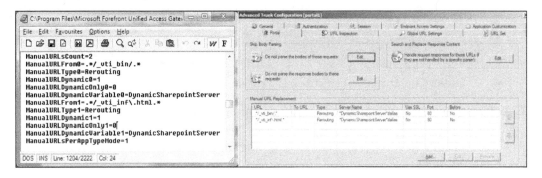

- `Image`: This path specifies the default image icon for the application.

- `ShortDesc`: The default short description that is shown on the portal. This text also appears in the application's settings on the **Portal link** tab.

- `LongDesc`: The default long description.

- `OpenNewPage`: The default setting for having the application open in a new browser window or tab.

- `CanBeInitialApp`: When set to 1, this will set the application created based on this template to allow the administrator to configure the application to be the initial app on the trunk. This defaults to **yes**, so set it to 0 to disallow.

- `AllowPostWithoutContentType`: Set the app to allow a POST without a content type HTTP header (this option can be changed in the **Web Settings** tab).

- `DefaultSchema`: Set the app to default to a backend server that uses HTTPS rather than HTTP.

SSL-VPN specific settings and configuration

When a template in `WizardDefaultParams.ini` is intended to be an SSL-VPN based application, it has to include the `SSLVpnTemplate` parameter, which specifies the name of the SSL-VPN template to be used from the `SSLVPNTemplates.xml` file. When using this mode, you also have the option of specifying additional parameters, which can later be used with the template itself. These are specified using the following format:

- `SSLVPNNumOfElements=<Number>`

- `SSLVPNElement<Number>ID=<ID>`

- `<ID>Name=<Name>`

- `<ID>Type=<type>`
- `<ID>GuiType=<GUI Type>`
- `<ID>Value=<Value>`
- `<ID>Validation=<Validation Parameter>`

The element name is simple text. The types available are:

- `0`: Textual server names
- `1`: Number
- `2`: Free text

The `GuiType` can be:

- `0`: Multiple lines for server names
- `1`: Single line for server name
- `2`: Multiple lines for server names
- `3`: Drop-down

When using the drop-down option, the possible values are specified with the `<ID>ListValue` parameter, separated by semicolons. The `<ID>GuiWidth` parameter specifies the size of the drop-down element.

The `Validation` element can be `NotEmpty`, `IP/DNS`, `Port`, `Pattern`, or a combination of the various elements. As you can guess, `IP/DNS` tells UAG to verify that the server specification can be resolved, and `Port` needs to be a numerical value between 1 and 65535 (although TCP/IP allows for port `0`, it's actually reserved, so cannot be used here). The pattern element specifies a RegEx pattern as follows:

```
<ID>Validation=Pattern(Exclude /:*?"<>|)
```

When creating a template, one can have any number of elements, and each element can have some or all of the parameters. Typically, the server and port parameters are pretty important, although not for every scenario. For instance, creating an app to run a script, such as the one discussed earlier, does not actually require any specific elements or parameters.

Tying in to the SSL-VPN template list

The structure of the templates in SSLVPNTemplates.xml is very diverse, and can do a lot of things. The most basic structure is as follows:

```
<template name="MyStuff" userrights="0" use-with-lsp="yes"
default="yes" >
<port id="0" remoteport="0" flags="514"/>
</template>
```

This specifies the name of the template (which the Wizard Default file refers to), and the TCP/IP ports used. In addition, the Template tag can also specify the use of the socket forwarder (use-with-lsp) and the default="yes" tag specifies that the application can be used with all platforms, as opposed to using win="yes", which limits it to Windows-based clients.

It's probably worth mentioning that a flag value of 514 actually places the tunnel component into **Simple Relay mode**, which in short opens a port on the client and tunnels the TCP traffic to the target application server. The actual listener port is created on the client and the SSL wrapper component takes care of making the necessary changes, such as changes to the application settings, registry or hosts file, in order for the application to communicate through this tunnel.

Several other modes exist and the flags you'll see defined in these elements have been calculated by the UAG product group using a special tool, which for security reasons is not available to the public.

You can also specify a config-file tag, and an exec tag, which define parameters to be retrieved from the application and used in creating and executing an executable. For example:

```
<template name="RunBatch" userrights="562" use-with-lsp="yes"
win="yes">
<port id="0" remoteport="139" flags="10" use-with-lsp="yes"/>
<config-file flags="1" path="%Temp%\CleanTemp.bat" use-with-lsp="yes">
<![CDATA[
del %temp%\*.*
]]>
</config-file>
<exec exe='%Temp%\CleanTemp.bat flags="4" param=""/>
</template>
```

The preceding code creates a batch file named `CleanTemp.bat` in the system's temporary folder and populates it with the command `del %temp%\*.*`. When that application is launched, it deletes the content of the system's `temp` folder, of course.

The template can also modify the registry, and display a message to the users:

```
<template name="MyApp" userrights="116" use-with-lsp="yes" win="yes">
<port id="0" flags="1" ip2relay="169.1.1.1" remoteport="111"/>
<config-file flags="32" path="" use-with-lsp="yes"><![CDATA[
[1\ Control Panel\Desktop]
ScreenSaveActive =1
]]>
</config-file>
<exec exe="\nScreen Saver Enabled" param="" flags="256"/>
</template>
```

The preceding application template, when launched, will set the registry value for `HKEY_CURRENT_USER\Control Panel\Desktop\ScreenSaveActive` to 1, enabling the screen saver on the client. The text specified in `exec` will be shown to the user.

Consider another example:

```
<exec exe="%CommandLine%" param="%CommandLineArguments%" flags="1032"
default="yes"/>
```

This tag will expect the application to deliver the parameters `CommandLine` and `CommandLineArguments`, and will execute them. The preceding code is taken from the **Enhanced Generic Client Application** template, which lets you specify these as part of the application configuration. Naturally, the `exe` attribute can also specify an executable to be run as follows:

```
<exec exe="mstsc.exe -v:%localip%:%localport% -w:%HRes% -h:%VRes%"
flags="4" param="" use-with-lsp="no"/>
```

The preceding code is part of the Remote Desktop group of applications, and instructs the client to launch the Remote Desktop Client `MSTSC.EXE`, with the parameters sent by the app for the hostname, port, and display resolution.

Summary

Is that all? Far from it! Both the `WizardDefaultParams` and `SSLVPNTemplates` files have hundreds of additional parameters and options, but unfortunately, we cannot document all of them here. With careful observation and analysis of the default files, though, we are sure you can decipher what else they can do. The things you can do with these applications are endless, and almost unlimited. Go and explore! In the next chapter, we will learn how to configure UAG to use certificate authentication and smartcards.

6
Custom Certificate Authentication

As we know, one of UAG's greatest features is its extensive support for such a wide range of authentication providers and schemes, probably making it one of the most agnostic SSL-VPN solutions in the market in terms of its integration capabilities. The options here are pretty comprehensive right out of the box, and UAG's intrinsic flexibility really takes things a step further, but one type of scheme that continues to become very popular in terms of offering a more secure and seamless user experience is **certificate authentication**.

This method has been around for many years now in IIS. There may be slight variations in the way this scheme is implemented, depending on circumstances and third-party vendor integrations, but you'll be pleased to know that UAG works on the same core principals in this scenario, which is simply to authenticate users through standard X.509 certificates.

Unfortunately, enabling certificate authentication is not possible directly in UAG's graphic user interface and, if required, involves some degree of customization.

In this chapter, we will explore this type of authentication and, in turn, learn how to configure it. This chapter will cover the following topics:

- Certificate authentication concepts and terminology
- Understanding the building blocks of certificate authentication for UAG
- The certificate authentication custom files
- Certificate authentication with KCD
- Troubleshooting certificate authentication

Before going into detail however, it's important to understand what UAG can and cannot do with certificates, as this topic is the source of much confusion out there. Let's look at the three main types of certificate-based configurations that can be used for authentication or securing access into UAG:

- **Client certificate authentication**: The topic covered in this chapter.

- **UAG certified endpoints**: This is an optional feature used to enhance security by enabling having UAG perform a certificate check, in addition to the normal form-based authentication. When enabled, users log in as usual but also get prompted by the browser to select a user certificate. To be clear, this is certificate validation, not authentication and you can read more about this at the following URL:

  ```
  http://blogs.technet.com/b/ben/archive/2011/09/28/uag-and-
  certificates.aspx
  ```

- **Endpoint certificate policies**: In short, this option uses a combination of custom detection code and policies to further secure access into UAG's web portal and applications. In this scenario, UAG relies on the endpoint components to query a client's user or machine store for a certificate that complies with the criteria set out in your custom code. The actual certificate integrity check is performed on client side and UAG uses the response to control access, or if preferred to also raise a client's status from default to **Privileged Access**. As with **Certified Endpoints**, this option is for certificate validation only and not authentication.

So although UAG can do certificate authentication, you should be aware that it does not provide any support for authenticating the backend application servers using client certificates, either directly or by delegation.

Certificate authentication concepts and terminologies

Conceptually, certificates are something that can be used to encrypt information or prove identity, whether of a client device, a service, or an actual person, but ultimately allowing one entity to trust another. In the context of UAG certificate authentication, we are focused more on the purpose of identity, as opposed to encryption itself.

It's very likely that you've already seen the many certificate types that exist for different purposes. So we'll not delve too much into the intricacies of PKI itself, but knowing how to differentiate between them is a fundamental part of being a UAG administrator.

For example, when you browse to your bank's website to manage your account, the bank's site will present a certificate to prove to you (via your browser) that it is indeed who you think it is, and not a spoof run by cyber criminals. In this website scenario, the type of certificate used is typically referred to as a **Web Server** type for server authentication purposes, and would usually comprise of several key usage attributes, such as digital signature, key encipherment, and data encipherment. It is the digital signature attribute on the certificate that allows a site's identity to be verified, as it will have been **digitally signed** by the issuing **Certificate Authority (CA)**, using the authority's private key.

A UAG portal configured for SSL would use the same type of Server Authentication certificate and clients would validate the site's identity when connecting to it. Whatever the site or address, users will immediately be warned if a site's integrity cannot be certified, but all being well this then forms the basis for creating a secure and encrypted connection between two entities, otherwise known as a **secure channel**.

On the other hand, certificates used for user authentication still follow the same concept of being digitally signed by a trusted authority, but they are of a different type and better known as *Smartcard Logon* and *Smartcard User*, and with a purpose of client authentication.

One advantage that makes using certificates for authentication more secure is that it removes the need for having to provide credentials, and thereby negates the risk of someone or something obtaining your username and password. As with most things, there are still risks to be considered, with the most obvious being the loss of a device, such as a laptop that contains your user certificates, but these concerns can then be mitigated by introducing additional protection, such as the integrated Bitlocker functionality, to restrict access into the device's OS.

Choosing to store user certificates on smartcards instead of on machines can add an even greater layer of security, as their self-containment makes them more resistant to compromise and they are less dependent on potentially vulnerable resources. In fact, smartcards should be de-facto for any organization considering this type of authentication because in this scenario, one factor authentication, which is something you know as your password, is replaced with **two-factor authentication (2FA)**. In the world of security, this is generally known as **strong authentication** or **multifactor authentication**, on the basis that it is *something you have* (Smartcard), together with *something you know* (PIN). Some of the more advanced smartcard derivatives also include **One Time Code (OTC)** functionality to protect against the standard alphanumeric PIN from being compromised.

You'll find many organizations already using certificates in one shape or another, and issuing digital certificates to users and corporate devices has become a standard practice. Provisioning of certificates is an area we will not cover in this book, but at a high level this will typically consist of automating certificate distribution through group policy or some other mechanism, such as the **Microsoft Forefront Identity Management 2010 (FIM)** solution.

Issued certificates are usually stored somewhere accessible to the OS and to applications, and this would normally be in either one of two places — a computer's **cryptographic store** or the microchip on a Smartcard as previously mentioned. Regardless of location, all certificates can be viewed and managed through the Windows MMC certificate snap-in, or from the command line using PowerShell or **Certutil** depending on the OS version. Certain browsers, such as Internet Explorer and Firefox, also allow for some simple management tasks, such as importing and exporting of certificates. Other non-Windows systems, such as Mac OS X have their own equivalents of these utilities, such as **keychain**, which we will not cover here, but you can read more about this at the following URL:

```
http://docs.info.apple.com/article.html?path=Mac/10.6/en/9082.html.
```

On a Windows system, the cryptographic store (Crypto Store for short) is split between three distinct areas and these are represented in the certificate MMC as separate containers:

- The current user store: All certificates stored here are personal and for individual users. This is a profile-centric container and each user account on a system will have its own user certificates. It is this container that holds the user certificates used for UAG certificate authentication.

- The computer store: This is where all system-level certificates are stored including machine/computer certificates, and contents of this store are visible to all users with read permissions. This container typically holds certificates, such as IPSEC certificates used for VPNs' or DirectAccess, but also those that can be checked by UAG's detection policies.

- The services store: This container holds certificates that are bound to individual services and is not used for UAG-related activities.

A question that tends to come up frequently is how Smartcard certificates are managed and whether there are any special requirements or considerations when used with UAG. Physically, the choice of the card itself and the hardware used to read it is endless, but the bottom line is that they all do pretty much the same thing. You'll now find that many newer laptops ship with a card slot directly incorporated into the body. For machines that don't have this, a more modern and common alternative to the basic USB reader is the key **FOB**, which is similar to a USB drive, but holds a micro smart card with the size of a SIM.

All modern versions of Windows from 2000 and onwards have a built-in application programming interface (API) for use with smartcards, and this is referred to as a **Cryptographic Service Provider (CSP)**. The CSP API will handle access to the reader and card so middleware is usually not necessary for anything other than resetting a lost PIN or adding additional certificates.

Viewing a smartcard's certificates is as easy as launching the normal certificate MMC, selecting the **Current User** container, and plugging in your card. All user certificates found on the smartcard will be enumerated and shown in the list, as if stored on the machine itself. At this point, there are no restrictions to see the certificates and their properties, but any attempt to access a certificate's private key will cause the CSP to prompt for a PIN. Submitting the PIN successfully unlocks the certificate and it is then accessible to whatever program that is requesting it.

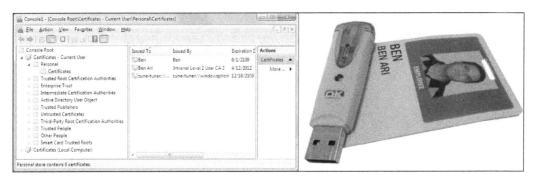

UAG and certificate authentication

Getting to grips with **Public Key Infrastructure (PKI)** can be a challenging task to say the least and it's certainly a subject we would encourage you to understand, but for now we'll assume you know your way around a Microsoft Enterprise Certificate Authority implementation.

It's from this server, whether a root CA or intermediate CA, that certificates will be issued and the two primary types that you're likely to see when working with UAG publishing and certificate authentication, are **user certificates** and **machine certificates** (also known as **computer certificates**). At a glance, they're not much different structurally, but in PKI terms, they serve different purposes. Their exact properties and usage scenarios can be observed through their respective source templates that reside on their issuing CA. Of the two, it is the user certificates that are required for this authentication scheme and the type of certificate template used to create these certificates on the CA is either Smartcard User or Smartcard Logon specifically. Both can be used for authentication, but the Smartcard User certificate can also be used for e-mail encryption, if required.

When a UAG server is configured for certificate authentication, users are forced to present a user certificate to UAG instead of submitting their credentials through UAG's login form. During this interaction, UAG will step through a sequence comprising of the following three key functions:

- UAG will verify that the client certificate integrity is valid
- UAG will perform a mapping of the certificate to the user account in Directory Services or any other defined LDAP server
- UAG will authenticate the user

At the core, UAG relies on the existing IIS 7.0 certificate authentication mechanism to facilitate this process, so key principals still remain. For instance, a prerequisite for this scheme to function is that the trunk that is configured for this is HTTPS and not HTTP.

To implement certificate authentication, you will need to configure UAG with a set of custom files, which basically forces it to request a user certificate, and to use the data from it to authenticate the user against the repository configured on the trunk. These files are as follows:

- `Cert.inc`
- `Login.inc`
- `Validate.inc`
- `Repository.inc`

The following link is Microsoft's official documentation for client certificate authentication with UAG and describes the procedure to implement this customization:

`http://technet.microsoft.com/en-us/library/ee861163.aspx`.

Basically, it involves copying four files from one of the code sample folders on UAG into another folder, and renaming them according to the standard file naming convention for UAG customizations. Then certain parameters need to be edited in the files to allow them to do their job. Documentations or guides, however, may be unclear, as they cover both the use of a *soft* certificate (one that is installed on the computer itself) and a Smartcard certificate. To add to the confusion, the instructions also attempt to cover three common certificate configurations, but do not explain the difference between them or how exactly they affect the content of the file.

We mentioned earlier that UAG retrieves certain values from the certificate and uses those values for authentication. The code you define within these files is what will depict which properties we query on the certificate explicitly, and in turn which **Active Directory (AD)** attributes are also queried when cross referencing the certificate data. For example, some organizations set their certificates to include the user's e-mail address (john.doe@createhive.com), while others are happy with the **User Principle Name (UPN)**, such as jdoe@createhive.local, or **Distinguished Name (DN)**, such as CN=John Doe,CN=Users,DC=createhive,DC=local.

It's imperative that you fully understand the differences between these naming conventions so as to provide the very best authentication and authorization solution design for any future projects.

If the identity is a username or e-mail, then it is typically stored in the **Subject** field of a certificate. However, if it is a UPN, then it will usually be stored in the **Subject Alternative Name (SAN)** field instead, or in addition to the subject if it already exists. Technically, there could be infinite variations to the preceding, and many organizations use custom certificate templates that could be drastically different. In other words, be prepared to deal with any situation, and keep an open mind.

Things can get even more complicated, as the retrieved values are verified against a **directory**, which may also have certain variations. Organizations using Active Directory would often store the user's username in the **SAM-Account-Name (sAMAccountName)** attribute, and would need to compare the username value retrieved from the certificate to that attribute. If the organization has selected to use a UPN or e-mail name as the key identity value, then it would probably compare it to the UPN or mail attributes in the directory. Some organizations use a different type of directory, such as Novell, SUN, or perhaps even a totally different mechanism to store user info. For example, the directory may be a custom SQL database, or even a flat text file. We will discuss custom repositories in the next chapter, but the important thing to bear in mind here is that every environment is different, and successfully configuring UAG for Certificate Authentication can be diverse and somewhat challenging.

Understanding the pieces of cert authentication for UAG

As already mentioned, the required customizations are based on four key files found in the following location:

```
<UAG Path>/von/conf/InternalSite/samples
```

The instructions ask you to perform the following steps:

1. Copy the file `site_secure_smartcard_cert.inc` from the `samples` folder to the `<UAG Path>/von/conf/InternalSite/inc/CustomUpdate`. You are then required to rename the file to `<trunk>1cert.inc`.

2. Copy the file `site_secure_login_for_cert.inc` from the `samples` folder to the `CustomUpdate` folder. You are then required to rename the file to `<trunk>1login.inc`.

3. Copy the file `site_secure_validate_for_cert.inc` from the `samples` folder to the `CustomUpdate` folder. You are then required to rename the file to `<trunk>1validate.inc`.

4. Copy the file `repository_for_cert.inc` from the `samples` folder to the `CustomUpdate` folder. You are then required to rename the file to `<repository>.inc`. Where `<repository>` is the name of your authentication repository as defined exactly in UAG's *Authentication and Authorization Servers* interface followed by a `1` for an HTTPS trunk, and then by the file name and extension. For example, when copying the `site_secure_cert.inc` file for an HTTPS trunk named `RemoteAccess`, the resulting file would be named `RemoteAccess1cert.inc`.

Note that the `1` in the filename indicates this is an HTTPS trunk. Normally, custom files are named with either `0` or `1` to indicate the type of trunk, but in this case, a trunk has to be HTTPS, so it will always be `1`.

In addition to copying them, some of the files require certain changes to work. Here are some more details about the files and what they do, so let's see how they are built and what their functions are.

Cert.inc

The cert.inc file actually comes as two separate files, with the first being site_secure_cert which can be used for both soft certs stored locally on machines and also for those stored on smartcards. The other file, site_secure_smartcard_cert.inc, contains the same code that defines the parameter that will be checked, but with one addition—it also checks that the certificate is of the Smartcard User or Smartcard Logon type before authenticating the user.

It does this by simply looking for the certificate **Enhanced Key Usage** (EKU) attribute, and when found, then continues to look for the smartcard **Object Identifier** (**OID**), which is 1.3.6.1.4.1.311.20.2.2. Once the user selects or confirms a certificate, its data is sent to the UAG server, where it will attempt to parse its properties. In the case of a smartcard certificate, the custom cert.inc will have been used to obtain the required certificate data for UAG to begin authenticating the user. The sample file site_secure_smartcard_cert.inc contains various variable constants that pertain to certain standard fields that most certificates have. For example, field code 7 represents the subject name field.

The actual code uses the COM object Microsoft.UAG.CertificateComHelper to query the certificate data and parse it. For this file to work, you need to specify the name of the **Certificate** field that is to be used and as illustrated previously, this is determined in line 64 which reads as follows:

```
upn = objCert.GetInfo(INFO_SUBJECT_UPN)
```

In addition, you need to edit the subject array settings at the bottom of the file (lines 91 to 98), which define the field selection for the next stages of the authentication. The default sample file is set for `SubjectEMAIL`, which is appropriate if you choose to use the e-mail attribute on certificates when authenticating users, but if you prefer the user's **Canonical Name** (**CN**) instead, then comment out line 92, and uncomment line 98 as shown in the following screenshot:

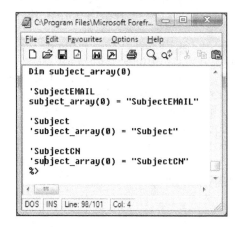

Please note that the line numbers referred to in this chapter may change in future updates to UAG, so should be used as examples only.

Login.inc

The file `<trunk>1login.inc` is designed to carry out two primary functions. The first is to redirect users to the mobile portal, if the client is detected as a mobile platform and cannot be authenticated by certificates. The second is to initiate the certificate authentication mechanism by forcing the client to redirect to the `cert.asp` file, instead of the default login page. Fortunately, it requires no changes other than naming it properly.

Validate.inc

The file `<trunk><1>validate.inc` is designed to tell UAG the name of the repository to be used for the certificate authentication. The only change required for it is to edit line 6 in the file, and type the name of the repository that is assigned to the trunk there as shown in the following screenshot:

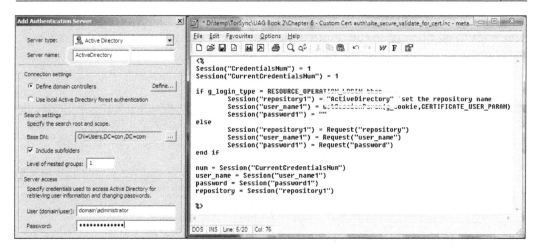

Repository.inc

One of the primary roles of this file `<repository>.inc` is to create the COM object required to return the results of the `AuthenticateRepositoryUser` function to the calling code in `<UAG Path>/von/conf/InternalSite/Validate.asp`.

This file is the most important part of the process and may require some changes. By default, the file is configured to retrieve the value of the **SubjectEMAIL** field from the certificate, and compare it against the `email` attribute in the repository. Depending on your own requirements and configuration, you may need to change this. However, the default file is not very well annotated, so we have prepared another version of the same file, but with some more notes for you to read.

We realize that even with the notes, the file is still high-level ASP code and may be challenging to fully understand, of course. To make things simpler, here are some of the things you might need to change.

If the field in the certificate that you need to retrieve is other than **SubjectEmail**, then you need to edit line 30 in the original file (line 64 in our version). This line reads as follows:

```
param_email.Name = "SubjectEMAIL"
```

If the attribute in the repository that you wish to compare against is not email, you need to edit line 61 in the original file (line 121 in our version). This line reads as follows:

```
param_email.Name = "mail"
```

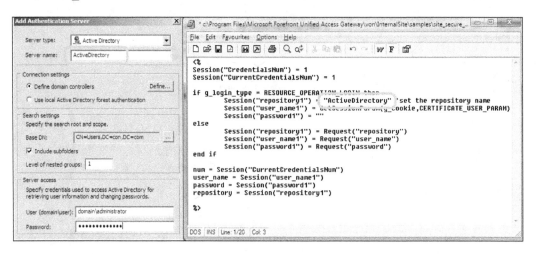

Certificate authentication with KCD

It's not uncommon for the Kerberos Constrained Delegation (KCD) authentication to be required in this scenario, which is why the custom repository.inc file contains specific code for this. The reason being, the users will no doubt want Single Sign On (SSO) access into applications that are being launched from the UAG portal or directly, but the fact is that logging in using certificates means that users never actually submit their username and password. So consequently, UAG does not have a cached set of user credentials to perform standard 401 or form-based authentication into applications. Instead, it must rely on obtaining a Kerberos token on behalf of the user, by means of delegation. Naturally, this requires that applications are configured for integrated Windows authentication, and at the same time that each published application in UAG is correctly configured with an Service Principal Name (SPN). Applications that are not configured for Kerberos authentication can be left to Basic or forms, and SSO for these applications can be disabled in UAG. The result is that the users will be challenged for authentication upon launching the application. However, if KCD is to be used, you will need to change line 3 in the repository.inc file, which reads KCDAuthentication_on = false, to read KCDAuthentication_on = true.

For doing this, you may also need to change how Kerberos performs authentication to application servers and the following registry change:

1. On the Forefront UAG server, run `Regedit`.

2. Navigate to `HKEY_LOCAL_MACHINE\SOFTWARE\WhaleCom\e-Gap\von\UrlFilter`.

3. Modify or create the `DWORD` value `KCDUseUPN` as follows:

   ° To perform authentication using UPN, set the `DWORD` value to `1`.

   ° To perform authentication using the format `domain\username`, set the DWORD value to `0`. If no value is set, `domain\username` will be used.

4. Exit the registry editor and activate your configuration to have the new setting saved (and applied to other array members, if relevant)

The following are the prerequisites for a KCD SSO configuration:

- The UAG server must be a domain member

- Domain controllers must all be Windows Server 2003 or later

- Only one authentication repository can be configured for the trunk to which the application belongs

- Users, UAG servers, and application servers must be part of the same domain

If all of these are met then you are good to go ahead and set things up. This involves creating SPN records that need to be added to computer accounts in Directory Services. More information on setting up SPN records and delegation, specifically for UAG, can be found at the following URL:

`http://technet.microsoft.com/en-us/library/ee690462.aspx`

Also, extended info can be found at the following URL:

`http://msdn.microsoft.com/en-us/library/aa480585.aspx`

Beyond that, the default code should do the trick, but if you made changes for other values and attributes, as we discussed earlier, you may need to adjust the functions some more.

Troubleshooting certificate authentication

As noted earlier, many real-world certificate authentication deployments are far from trivial, and it's always possible that the code changes that you have applied to achieve a more customized implementation do not work as expected.

Of all the issues we've seen and heard of while working on this subject, there is one that system admins are always guaranteed to fall upon. This is probably more of a gotcha than an issue and you'll encounter this when testing through a browser that is configured not to show the certificate selection pop-up, if only a single certificate is found. In this case, you may need to disable the "Don't prompt for client certificates" selection setting in IE's zone settings. Configure this as follows:

1. Open the settings for Internet Explorer.
2. Go to the **Security** tab.
3. Double-click the zone you wish to edit.
4. Scroll down to **Security**, and set the option as shown in the following screenshot:

We'd then suggest using UAG's good old tracing to drill right down into where things might be failing, and as you may have noticed, the code already includes quite a few function calls (`LIGHT_TRACE` and `HEAVY_TRACE`), which will prove invaluable.

In *Chapter 1*, *Customization Building Blocks*, we discussed the topic of performing enhanced tracing (also known as **InternalSite tracing**), which includes the output of these tracing functions. When troubleshooting certificate authentication, this type of tracing would be your friend. Run such a trace while reproducing your failed authentication or other issue, and in the resulting trace file, look for the output of the trace functions. For example, line 108 in the original `repository.inc` will log the following error, if it failed to match the retrieved user ID to the repository:

```
The session param [UPN] value [JohnDoe] is different from the user
param [JaneDoe]
```

```
for j = 0 to UBound(session_params)
        param_ok = false
        for i = 0 to UBound(user_params)
                if KCDAuthentication_on = false OR user_params(i).Name <> param_UPN.Name then
                        if session_params(j).Value = user_params(i).Value then 'Comparison is case sensitive
                                param_ok = true
                                exit for
                        else
                                LIGHT_TRACE "The session param [" & session_params(j).Name & "] value [" &_
                                'session_params(j).Value & "] is different from the user param [" & user_params(i).Value & "]"
                        end if
                end if
        next
```

We wish we could promise you things are going to be simple but they might not. If things don't make a lot of sense, another useful tool is LDP, which comes with the Windows Server 2003 support tools, but is also preinstalled on any system running UAG, TMG, or as a domain controller. This tool can query Active Directory and retrieve the various attributes a user may have, so you can fully understand what data exists in there, and what to expect the certificate authentication code in UAG to get from it. Another alternative is to use the integrated attribute editor, which is part of the user management console in Windows 2008 R2:

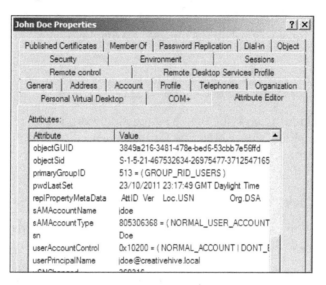

If everything is configured correctly for SSO using KCD, then you should expect to see the following sequence and exchanges between UAG, domain controllers, and the backend application server when tracing with Netmon or Wireshark:

1. UAG makes request to the target application server.
2. The Application server responds with authentication using negotiation.
3. A Kerberos token is requested from UAG to Ticket Granting Service (TGS) for the website (SPN) and on behalf of user.
4. The DC issues a Kerberos token to UAG server.
5. UAG presents the Kerberos token to the site.
6. The website authenticates the user.

Although seemingly straightforward, Kerberos can be pretty complex, so we would suggest keeping things as simple as possible when trying to troubleshoot, as this will increase your chances of quickly isolating any discrepancies. A good tip when doing this would be to test SSO against a simple IIS website that is configured for integrated authentication, but by using the host's FQDN instead of an alternative host header. The advantage of doing this is that an SPN configuration will already exist for a host's FDQN, so proving KCD actually works in the first instance can be quick and easy.

UAG's web monitor also provides some useful output by reporting whether or not it has been able to retrieve a token for the user by displaying a message similar to the following one:

```
"The S4U2Self Kerberos token for user johndoe with source IP address
80.195.11.110 was retrieved successfully"
```

If you struggle to identify an issue then a suggestion would be to try the IIS-based DelegConfig tool, which is very effective for troubleshooting and provides comprehensive output of findings. More information on this can be found at the following URL:

```
http://www.iis.net/community/default.aspx?tabid=34&g=6&i=1887.
```

Finally, for those who prefer something from a more familiar source is Jim Harrison's more basic version, which does an equally good job and can be found at the following URL:

```
http://isatools.org/tools/AuthTest.asp.txt.
```

Summary

This chapter explored the process of configuring UAG for certificate authentication by using the sample files included with UAG, and adapting them to your needs. This serves as the basis for the topic covered in the next chapter—Creating your own custom repository, which is a lot more challenging, but also provides incredible benefits by allowing you to authenticate your users against virtually any directory.

7
Custom Authentication Repositories

One of the strongest points of UAG is its ability to authenticate users against many types of authentication providers. While most customers use **Active Directory** and Active Directory only, many require other or additional providers, such as **RSA SecureID** or **LDAP**. However, with some customizations you can also define your own custom authentication. This could be almost anything—an SQL database, for example, is one popular customization, but other options are available. In this chapter, we will discuss the following topics:

- How does custom authentication work?
- Verifying usernames
- Working with an SQL database
- More elaborate code
- Testing and debugging your code
- Putting it all together

How does custom authentication work?

The process of authentication with UAG includes three key pieces:

- UAG presents the login form to the user and collects the credentials
- UAG verifies the credentials against the defined authentication repository or repositories, defined on the trunk
- UAG stores the credentials and reuses them when single sign on (SSO) is required, such as when launching a published application

To do this, the login form (`login.asp`) contains the fields that are to be collected. Once the form is submitted, the validation page (`validate.asp`) is called, and it verifies the credentials against the selected repository or repositories. The following diagram illustrates the authentication flow and the various functions that UAG will step through when authenticating users against a repository:

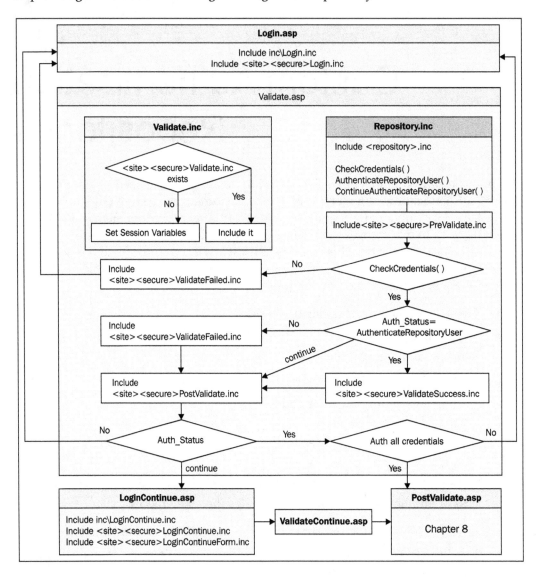

The processes that go on afterwards are less relevant here, but will be discussed in the next chapter.

The actual validation is handled by a single file, often referred to as `repository.inc`, although your own filename will be different. This file needs to contain a single function, which compares the data provided by the user to whatever data source you want to use, and outputs either a success or failure object. It can contain supporting functions as well, of course, but the core functionality is the authentication function, detailed as follows.

The following screenshot is a sample of a very simple authentication function:

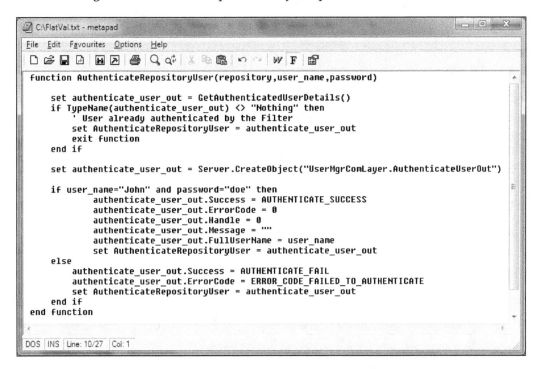

This sample, of course, is not going to go very far, if you notice what's going on in line 12 (`if user_name="John" and password="doe" then`). Basically, this will allow access only to a user named `John`, with the password `doe`. However, this illustrates the concept. The primary function `AuthenticateRepositoryUser` gets called from line 74 in the page `/InternalSite/validate.asp` and the caller will provide the credentials that the user typed in on the logon page.

First, we execute the function `GetAuthenticatedUserDetails`, which would return empty if the user has already authenticated.

If the user has not authenticated yet, we use the `UserMgrComLayer` object to create the `AuthenticateUserOut` object, and do some checking of the provided username and password. If the checking is successful, we set some properties of the object, most notably `authenticate_user_out.Success` with the constant `AUTHENTICATE_SUCCESS`, and set the function's return with the content of that object (lines 18 or 22 above).

The structure is pretty simple, and the important bit is the `If/Then` statement that's in the lower half of the preceding sample. This is where the magic happens and you can put in any ASP code that you want to use as your verification process.

Verifying usernames

The process of user and password verification is where the real power of ASP comes into play. You can compare a user's submitted credentials to literally any information store that offers a query interface, and that you know how to interact with. The Windows Operating System comes prepopulated with a huge selection of COM objects, which you can utilize to interact with your data source. The simplest example is the `FileSystemObject`, which allows you to read files directly from the server's hard drive.

For example, consider the following screenshot:

```
set FSO = server.createObject("Scripting.FileSystemObject")
Filepath = Server.MapPath("users.txt")
if FSO.FileExists(Filepath) Then
        Set UserFile = fso.OpenTextFile(Filepath)
        UserList=split(content.readAll,";")
        for i = 0 to ubound(UserList)
                if UserList(i)=user_name & "%" & password then
                        'Run successful auth code
                end if
        next
        if authenticate_user_out.Success <> AUTHENTICATE_SUCCESS then
                'Run failed auth code
        end if
Else
        Response.redirect "/InternalSite/CustomUpdate/Error.asp?id=1"
End If
Set FSO = nothing
```

The preceding sample is not UAG-specific, but rather just simple ASP code to read a file off the hard drive and parse its contents to look for the username and password. In the preceding code, we read the flat text file `users.txt`, which is a semicolon-separated list of user+password combinations formatted as `user%password`. We read the content of the file into a variable, and then use the `split` command to convert that list into an array. We then go through the array, member by member, and compare the values to get a successful authentication. If none of the users match, we leave the function with the fail code, similar to what we used earlier.

Alternatively, one can use the `ReadLine` method, and go through a user list file where each line contains a username and password set. Whatever code you write or use depends mostly on your creativity, and your comfort level with writing and testing ASP code.

Working with an SQL database

One of the more popular custom repositories uses SQL as its database, and this is also pretty easy, as SQL has built-in functions for effective searching, even if the database contains a huge number of users. To interact with SQL, Windows offers the built-in **ADODB** object. All you have to do is initialize it, and create an SQL `Select` query to poll the user's name and password from SQL.

The following screenshot shows the sample code:

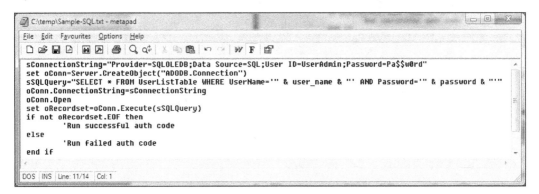

The code defines the name of the SQL server, DB name, and the SQL user which has access to the user's list table. It then creates an SQL query to select the table rows that match the user's username and password, and executes the query. After this, if the resulting collection is not empty, it means that at least one record matches both the username and password, and that's what we want. Otherwise, there is no match and the authentication fails.

The preceding example is far from programming best practices as it is not very secure, due to the database's user being hardcoded into the code, and listed in plain text. For our example this is good enough, though in real-world deployments, a better approach would be to use the **ODBC** administrative tool to create the DB connection (also known as a **DSN**), and then just call it from the code. This way, the user credentials are not shown, and if you change the username or password, you can simply edit the DSN settings, instead of the code itself as shown in the following screenshot:

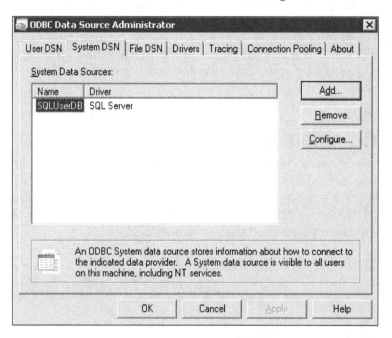

There are countless guides and articles out there which discuss using ASP code to interact with a database. One of the nice things about the ADODB object is that it can just as easily interact with an Oracle DB, a local access (MDB) file, or even an Excel file. The following article lists connection strings for popular data sources:

`http://support.microsoft.com/kb/300382.`

More elaborate code

Other than SQL and other databases, you can create a custom repository to interact with pretty much anything. We already mentioned that you can interact with any COM API that is built into Windows, and another such example is **ServerXMLHTTP**, which allows your ASP code to interact directly with web servers. You can use it to send GET and POST requests, and retrieve the response body or headers.

In fact, you are not limited to just built-in objects. This is one of the wonderful things about COM objects—any system that has a COM API can be used. This may entail installing some client software on the UAG server, or simply registering a DLL file. Most authentication providers in the world are LDAP-compliant (such as Sun iPlanet or Novell NDS). However, if you have another, as long as it has an ASP-compatible COM object, it's mostly a matter of learning how to interact with it.

One aspect of processing a user's credentials is the fact that username formatting can vary. Some organizations prefer that their users use the common domain\username format when logging in, while others may prefer the username@domain format (also referred to as UPN). Many systems, such as Exchange, are designed to support either of those automatically, but your custom repository will not do so automatically. Before writing your code, it's vital that you understand what users prefer to use as a format, as it's not always obvious, and at the same time habits can change, so make sure your code is as agnostic as possible. Ideally, it would be able to handle any possible option.

Consider the following screenshot for example:

```
sWhereSlash = InStr(user_name, "\")
if sWhereSlash = 0 then
        sWhereSlash = InStr(user_name, "/")
end if
if sWhereSlash > 0 then
        sDomain = Left(user_name, sWhereSlash - 1)
        sUserName = Mid(user_name, sWhereSlash + 1)
else
        sWhereAt = InStr(user_name, "@")
        if sWhereAt > 0 then
                sDomain = Mid(user_name, sWhereAt + 1)
                sUserName  = Left(user_name, sWhereAt - 1)
        else
                sDomain = "DefaultDomain"
                sUserName = user_name
        end if
end if
```

The preceding code accommodates all options—it starts by looking for either a forward or backslash (domain\user or domain/user), and if it doesn't find this format, looks for the @ sign. If this comes up empty as well, it will deduce the user simply fed in a username with no domain at all, and will populate the sDomain variable with the organization's default domain name.

Testing and debugging your code

One of the challenges of doing this kind of work is testing and debugging. We haven't discussed how to actually integrate the code with the UAG portal, but we will go through that soon. At some point you will have to create the custom files and do a real test with a browser connecting to the UAG trunk. However, before getting there, you better start with simple testing. If you were to do the testing with a *real* client, you will probably waste a lot of time, as the effort of reconnecting to the portal on each fix-and-retry, not to mention the time it takes for the activation to complete are a real hassle.

To out help comes **CSCRIPT**, the VBScript interpreter that is built into Windows. All you have to do is write your credential verification code as a standalone file, and save it somewhere with a `.VBS` extension. Then, configure Windows to execute the script using the CSCRIPT engine by running the following command in an administrative command prompt:

```
Cscript //h:cscript
```

Now, run your script, and if there's anything wrong, you will receive an error indicating what's up. If it's not an error, but some bug, you can also use the `wscript.echo` command to provide you with visual feedback about the progress of the script. Here are additional things you need to keep in mind:

- With VBS files, you don't need to start and end your code with `<%` and `%>`
- With VBS files, you initialize an object with `CreateObject` and not `Server.CreateObject`
- If you are referring to local files on the system, you cannot use the `Server.MapPath` method, but need to define the path fully

For example, this is how the SQL sample code from earlier would look when written as a VBS with debug output:

```
C:\temp\TestAuth.vbs - metapad                                                    □ ▣ 〓
File  Edit  Favourites  Options  Help
  □ ☞ 🖫 🗋  🖫 🖻  🖨  🔍 🔍  ✂  🗈 🖺  ↺ ↻  w  F  🗗

wscript.echo "Starting authentication test"
Results = AuthenticateRepositoryUser("NoMatter","john","doe")
wscript.echo Results.Success

function AuthenticateRepositoryUser(repository,user_name,password)
        wscript.echo "Checking if the user is authenticated already"
        set authenticate_user_out = GetAuthenticatedUserDetails()
        if TypeName(authenticate_user_out) <> "Nothing" then
                set AuthenticateRepositoryUser = authenticate_user_out
                wscript.echo "User is already authenticated. Exiting function"
                exit function
        end if
        wscript.echo "User is not authenticated. Defining SQL provider and creating object"
        sConnectionString="Provider=SQLOLEDB;Data Source=SQL;User ID=UserAdmin;Password=Pa$$w0rd"
        set oConn=CreateObject("ADODB.Connection")
        wscript.echo "Defining SQL query and opening connection"
        sSQLQuery="SELECT * FROM UserListTable WHERE UserName='" & user_name & "' AND Password='" & password & "'"
        oConn.ConnectionString=sConnectionString
        oConn.Open
        wscript.echo "Executing SQL Query"
        set oRecordset=oConn.Execute(sSQLQuery)
        wscript.echo "Checking if results returned"
        if not oRecordset.EOF then
                wscript.echo "Found user - auth successful!"
                authenticate_user_out.Success = AUTHENTICATE_SUCCESS
                authenticate_user_out.ErrorCode = 0
                authenticate_user_out.Handle = 0
                authenticate_user_out.Message = ""
                authenticate_user_out.FullUserName = user_name
        else
                wscript.echo "User not found - auth failed!"
                authenticate_user_out.Success = AUTHENTICATE_FAIL
                authenticate_user_out.ErrorCode = ERROR_CODE_FAILED_TO_AUTHENTICATE
        end if
        wscript.echo "Ending function and returning"
        set AuthenticateRepositoryUser = authenticate_user_out
end function
DOS  INS  Line: 32/39  Col: 35
```

Once this passes successfully without any bugs, you can continue to the next step of creating an actual repository from this code, but keep in mind that when the code is deployed, you may need to do additional debugging. For this, you might want to implement some tracing. As you may recall from the previous chapters, this involves adding lines such as the following to the code:

```
HEAVY_TRACE "Error processing user name " & user_name
```

You can add as many of those as you want, and they have no effect on server performance, so tracing as much info as possible is a good idea. If your code is misbehaving, you can enable tracing using the UAG Trace tool, and the trace will show the info that was collected during the session.

Putting it all together

Once your code is ready, the next step is putting it all together. This is actually a rather simple process. Make sure your code is formatted correctly:

- Get rid of the `wscript.echo` commands or replace them with trace commands
- Make sure the file starts and ends with `<%` and `%>`
- Make sure objects are initialized with `server.createobject`
- Make sure the code is within one of the UAG-specific repository functions, such as `AuthenticateRepositoryUser`
- Verify if the code handles the credentials received as parameters of the function, unlike in the VBScript
- Potentially, the code may need to use some other UAG specifics, such as UAG session variables, which would not be available in a test VBS
- Save the file under `/InternalSite/inc/CustomUpdate` with a name of your choice, and the extension `.INC`

Note that the name you will choose for the file will be the name you define as the repository's name in the UAG user interface, so it would be a good idea to have one that makes sense.

Once the file is there, follow these steps:

1. Launch UAG's management console and from the **Admin** menu head into **Authentication and Authorization Servers**.
2. Click on **Add Authentication Server** to create a new repository.
3. From the drop-down of the repository type, select **Other**.
4. Type a name for the repository that matches the name you gave your INC file (just the filename, without the extension!).
5. Click on **OK**.
6. Configure your trunk and applications with the new repository.
7. Activate the UAG configuration.
8. Test everything!

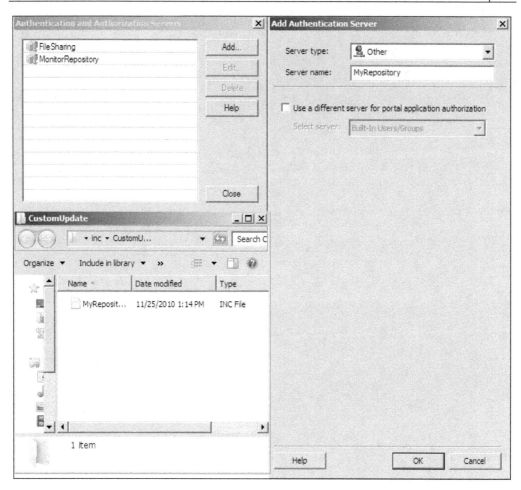

Summary

As always, this is just the beginning, as the things you can do with a custom repository are amazing. By integrating a custom repository with other repositories, you can do even more advanced things, such as working with OTP authentication or Certificates. The only limit is your imagination. To help facilitate more ideas, we recommend looking at the five sample files that are in `<UAG Folder>\Von\InternalSite\Samples`, which contains several other interesting functions that can allow UAG to interact with various information sources. In the next chapter, we will look into things you can do post authentication, and that's when things really become crazy....crazily awesome, that is!

8
Extending the Login Process with Customization

For the end user, everything starts with logging in to the UAG portal, but that doesn't mean it ends there. Like most of UAG's functionalities, the login process code is open and accessible to the administrator, and that allows you to integrate a special kind of magic into it. In this chapter, we will discuss the following topics:

- The UAG authentication flow
- Creating a Post Post Validate file
- Integrating your own code and interacting with UAG's COM object
- Putting data into the session
- Adding parameters
- Sending data to the backend server
- More ideas

The UAG authentication flow

The UAG authentication flow actually starts before the logon page is seen by the user. As the browser calls the initial trunk URL, UAG automatically directs the user to a page that initializes the session parameters (Initparams.aspx) in case the user does not yet have an existing session. Once a session is initiated, UAG attempts to detect the presence of its endpoint components on the client, and if they do not yet exist, they are offered to the user through the normal Active-X installation dialogs. Only then is the user sent to the login page, following their decision to allow component installation, or decline and continue with limited functionality (web application publishing only and also no socket forwarding, no SSTP or network connector, no endpoint detection, and no endpoint-cleanup).

While the preceding info is not directly related to authentication, it's important to know that information collected during this phase can be vital to what then follows, and ultimately to how UAG then applies its access controls and security policies. For example, UAG may have been configured to block access to all Windows platforms, such as Macintosh computers, and so users connecting from a Mac OS will be sent an access-denied page instead of the regular login page. So in terms of customizations, it's all very well adding code here and there to achieve whatever, but as a general rule, you should always fully evaluate your approach and plan carefully. Particularly when your work involves authentication! Of course there are other examples, but the point we're making is that it's important to understand UAG's flow and mechanisms as each component can have a great influence over another. As you can see from the flow diagram in the previous chapter, there are many files and hooks that make up the authentication process and those are really the ones you need to know, but for anyone more curious and interested in mapping things out a little, the following is the complete list:

Hook file	Calling file
Login.inc	Login.asp
LoginForm.inc	Login.asp
PreValidate.inc	Validate.asp
ValidateSuccess.inc	Validate.asp
ValidateFailed.inc	Validate.asp
PostValidate.inc	Validate.asp
LoginChangePassword.inc	LoginChangePassword.asp
LoginChangePasswordForm.inc	LoginChangePassword.asp
PreValidateChangePassword.inc	ValidateChangePassword.asp
ValidateChangePassword.inc	ValidateChangePassword.asp
ValidateChangePasswordSuccess.inc	ValidateChangePassword.asp
ValidateChangePasswordFailed.inc	ValidateChangePassword.asp
PostValidateChangePassword.inc	ValidateChangePassword.asp
LoginContinue.inc	LoginContinue.asp
LoginContinueForm.inc	LoginContinue.asp
PreValidateContinue.inc	ValidateContinue.asp
ValidateContinueSuccess.inc	ValidateContinue.asp
ValidateContinueFailed.inc	ValidateContinue.asp

Hook file	Calling file
`PostValidateContinue.inc`	`ValidateContinue.asp`
`PrePostValidate.inc`	`PostValidate.asp`
`PostPostValidate.inc`	`PostValidate.asp`
`LoginChooseUser.inc`	`LoginChooseUser.asp`
`LoginChooseUserForm.inc`	`LoginChooseUser.asp`
`Notes.inc`	`Notes.asp`

As far as users are concerned, they are completely oblivious to what goes on during the login sequence, as UAG obfuscates most of this and even hides the real filenames from being shown in the browser's address bar, to only show `PortalHomePage`.

Once the user has reached the login page and submitted their credentials, UAG calls the validation page (`validate.asp`), which then calls several other INC files such as `repository.inc`, which we discussed in the previous two chapters. Then once validation has completed successfully, the `RedirectToOrigUrl.asp` page takes care of sending the user back to the URL they originally typed in.

As part of the validation process, UAG has a built-in hook for a process known as **Post Post Validate**. This is a call to a file which does not exist by default, but you can add it, and within it, run your own code, smack in the middle of the login process. In actual fact, UAG also has another customizable hook that gets called even earlier in the process and this is referred to as **Pre Validate**. Most of your time will be spent focusing on the later of these two but there are situations where you'll need to consider this instead. For instance, a simple use of Pre Validate might be to change the way in which a user's credentials are formatted before UAG tries to validate them. Or maybe just nice to have, such as adding some sort of CAPTCHA mechanism to the login page to mitigate against bot attacks. As you can see, there are definitely some good uses for this but it's the Post Post Validate that'll really keep you busy.

So at a high level this is how things flow, but now you know that UAG is actually doing a lot more in the background. Go ahead and take a look and you'll see that the validation process is not just a single page—it actually does call for multiple INC files as part of its routine, and that's where things get interesting.

When planning, the first few questions that you should be asking yourself are the following:

- What are you trying to achieve?
- How can you achieve this and where is the place to inject your code?
- Is it covered by Microsoft's supportability statement on UAG?
- How are you going to test this before going into production?

Once you have these worked out, you can then begin looking at the code itself. Essentially that's it and there's not much required other than creating an INC file in the right location, and within it you place the ASP code that runs after the authentication process is completed, and before the user is sent to the URL he wanted to go-to. The results are very effective and a simple post-validate hook could be used to send the user to a disclaimer page that stipulates the requirements or conditions to using your site and the applications it contains. However, it doesn't stop there. You can probably think of other uses, such as a portal FAQ or the like. The nice thing at this point is that the user already has an active session, and that session has the user's information, including any data collected during the endpoint detection process. This means that your code can take advantage of this for various purposes. For instance, just some of the many things you'll see before the user has logged in are their source IP address, computer name, computer's domain membership, and much more. If you so desire, you could even make decisions based on that information, such as redirecting the user to a certain application, or even a different UAG server altogether. The things you can do with this integration are amazing, so let's start exploring!

Creating a Post Post Validate file

To create a custom Post Post Validate file, follow these steps:

1. Navigate to `<UAG Path>\Von\InternalSite\Inc\CustomUpdate`.
2. Create a new text file in that folder.
3. Name the file according to your trunk name, type, and with the suffix of `postpostvalidate.inc`. As with most custom INC files, if you have named your trunk `UAGPortal`, and it is an HTTPS trunk, the resulting filename would be `UAGPortal1postpostvalidate.inc`. For an HTTP trunk, use `0` instead of `1`.
4. Create ASP code inside that file, enclosed in the standard `<% %>` structure.

Activating UAG is not required for this new file to be acknowledged and testing can be performed immediately, but whatever happens, be sure to activate at some point as the change will need to be pushed into the TMG storage and ultimately received by other members if you run an array.

Naturally, keeping the code bug-free is important, because if your code errors out, no one will be able to log in to the portal until you fix it, so always be careful. Standard debugging techniques we discussed in earlier chapters, such as enabling full error messages on the server and adding debug code (using the built-in HEAVY_TRACE functions) apply here as well.

Integrating your own code and interacting with UAG's COM object

Now that you have a file in place, let's see what you can do with it. The following is a simple example:

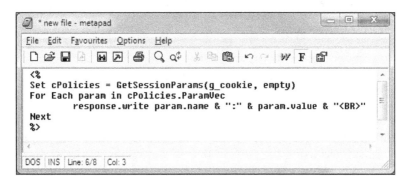

The preceding file does something rather simple, but amazingly powerful. It invokes the function GetSessionParams (which is located in \von\InternalSite\inc\SessionMgr.inc) to populate the cPolicies collection with the various parameters that were collected as part of the session. Then, the script uses a for-each loop to go through that collection, to print out the name of each parameter and its returned value. Since this piece of code runs right after a user has logged in, in the context of the user's session, this will simply print out a list of all parameters for that specific session.

Just consider the wealth of information these parameters contain and you'll soon realize the possibilities they offer and the fact that you can use them for some many different purposes. For example, you could use the response.redirect method to launch one of the portal applications if the computer is running a required service pack for your operating system of choice, or send them to a download page for that service pack if not.

Another thing that many users want to do is keep a log of the collected parameters, or at least some of them. UAG does keep a log of all sessions, but not of the session parameters. Using the `SystemFileObject` COM object, you could dump the entire list of values into a text file on the local hard drive, or maybe even run a SQL query to push this data straight into a database. The following is a code sample for dumping the parameters to a flat file on the UAG server:

```
<%
const intForWriting=2
Set cPolicies = GetSessionParams(g_cookie, empty)
strListParams = "<Table>"
For Each param in cPolicies.ParamVec
        strListParams = strListParams  & "<TR><TD>" & param.name & "</TD><TD>" & param.value & "</TD></TR>"
        if param.name = "Nonce" then
                strUniqueID = param.value
        end if
Next
strListParams = strListParams  & "</Table>"
strFileDate = Now
strFileDate = replace(strFileDate ,"/","-")
strFileDate = replace(strFileDate ,":","")
strFileName = "c:\temp\" & "SessionInfo-" & strUniqueID & strFileDate & ".log"
set FileObj = Server.CreateObject("scripting.FileSystemObject")
set SaveFile = FileObj.OpenTextFile(strFileName,intForWriting,True)
SaveFile.Writeline strListParams
SaveFile.Close
%>
```

The preceding code goes through the entire parameters collection (`cPolicies.ParamVec`) and for each of them builds an HTML table row containing the parameter name and value. It also looks for the parameter named **Nonce**, which stores the client's unique session ID. Once the loop is finished, the entire table is dumped into a text file that is named using the session ID and the system's current time and date. Simple huh? Doing this with SQL instead of a file would involve initializing the ADODB object, and building an `INSERT INTO` command with the value sets, followed by simply executing that command to store the session data into the table. One thing that's important to keep in mind is that the parameter list is pretty long and you should expect to be using-up about 15 KB per session. This doesn't sound like very much and particularly for today's hard drives or SQL databases that provide an abundance of storage space, but it does add up and if your server is very busy, it could accumulate to a significant amount of data. Also, if the server is heavily used, the additional effort in processing these transactions per login could have some impact on performance. A way to optimize this would be to collect just the parameters you actually need. For example, the list of parameters relating to AV products alone is somewhere around the 200 mark. It may be sufficient to collect only those relating to the AV products you permit, or maybe collecting just the `Installed` value and disregarding the `Running` and `UpToDate` values.

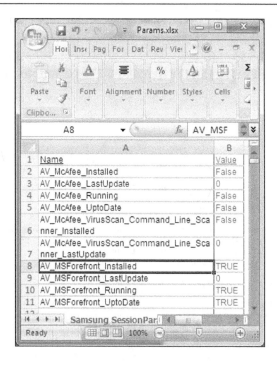

Putting data into the session

We just saw how you can retrieve session data, but in a similar fashion, you can also put your own data into the session. The following is a function that does that:

```
AddSessionUser g_cookie,"User","Password","Repository"
```

The function `AddSessionUser` resides in `\Von\InternalSite\Inc\SessionMgr.inc`, and as you've probably guessed, is used to add a user's submitted credentials into the session, so as to use them later for single sign on. By invoking this function ourselves in `PostPostValidate.inc`, we can also take advantage of this to add extra credentials into the session for any chosen repository. What would that be good for, do you ask? Well, one good example is when users are required to authenticate to an application that does not use the same repository that a trunk is configured with for initial login. In this scenario, the application would need credentials that it can expect to validate and authenticate against whatever directory or scheme it is configured with, and so those entered by the user at login would fail during SSO. To explain this further, users will typically have a primary set of credentials to log in to their domain, but might then also possess a different set altogether to access a restricted or isolated application that may not be domain integrated. Or another close situation is where an application expects the user's login ID to be in a different format to how it was entered by the user, and in turn stored in UAG's session cache for SSO.

This is a perfect example of where you could incorporate the necessary code to perform some rudimentary manipulation. In such a situation, you might have a database to store these specific credentials, and would use a simple SQL query with the ADODB object to handle the translation. For example, consider the following screenshot:

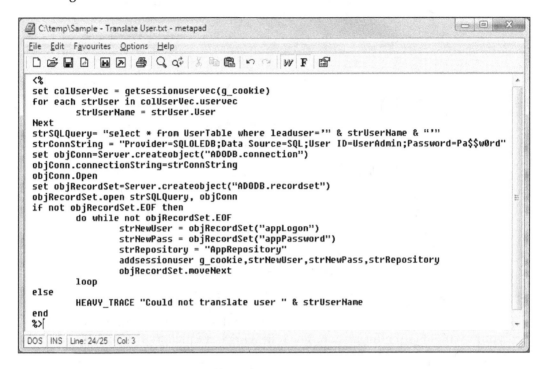

A much better solution would be to have your code encrypt the credentials in the database. However for the preceding example, we've kept it simple, and jump straight into retrieving the lead user associated with the session by using a `for-each` loop to extract the user ID from the collected session info. Then we issue an SQL query to see whether any rows in the table `UserTable` match that user ID. If found, we collect the credentials from the corresponding rows and add them to the session using the `AddSessionUser` function, or send a trace error if there were no matches.

It's important to remember that UAG will already do this by default for every user that authenticates to a trunk, where their credentials are added to the session and associated with the repository that was used to authenticate them. There are no limits on the amount of credentials that can be added to a client session, and equally on how many sets of credentials UAG can be associated with any repository, but you should be aware that associating more than one set of credentials to a repository will leave UAG prompting the user for which they would like to use for SSO.

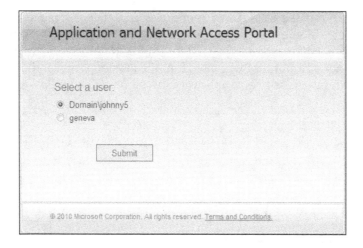

This is a standard behavior and the `LoginChooser.asp` file is responsible for controlling this. A suggestion for getting round this would be to create a new **Other** repository that would be used to hold our second set of credentials for and ultimately to perform SSO by adding it to the application's **Authentication** tab. As far as your INC file is concerned, you would just need to make sure `AddSessionUser` referenced the new repository.

This type of configuration is often referred to as using a *dummy* repository and you'll find that a similar configuration can also be applied to control access of applications through the **Authorization** tab. Nice and simple, wouldn't you agree?

Adding parameters

Another thing you can do with `PostPostValidate` is injecting your own information into the session parameters table. Normally, these are collected using the endpoint detection mechanism (we spoke about customizing that in *Chapter 3, Customizing Endpoint Detection and Policies*), but you can add more right here using the function `SetSessionParamWithType`. This function has the following syntax:

```
SetSessionParamWithType g_cookie, <Parameter Name>, <Parameter value>,
<type of parameter>
```

This function also resides in `\Von\InternalSite\Inc\SessionMgr.inc` and is used extensively by other code pieces.

This structure can be used to perform operations on data collected as part of the endpoint policy, or by the server itself, and then inject the results into the session itself. For instance, you can check the current time and convert the result to some flag or value. Once you put that flag back into the session, you can have the session policy allow or deny access to an application based on it. The following is the code for the same:

```
<%
intLoginTime = timer
if intLoginTime > 0 and intLoginTime< 32400 then
  bolNightSession = true
else
  bolNightSession = false
end if
SetSessionParamWithType g_cookie, "Night_Session", bolNightSession,
"Policy"
%>
```

This is useful if you want to control access to the server based on the time of day. The `timer` system variable returns an integer representing the server time in seconds, between 0 (midnight) and 86399 (one second before the next midnight). The preceding sample uses 32400, which is 9 AM. Naturally, you can perform other, more advanced calculations and gain unprecedented control over the policy, or collect very accurate data about server usage.

One specific trick many people are trying to work out is getting the user's IP. This parameter is actually collected by the endpoint detection script, but you cannot use it as part of an endpoint policy. This is with good reason, as the client's IP address is far too easy to spoof to serve for any serious security filtering. If, however, you need it for a more academic or less serious use, you can use `PostPostValidate` to convert the parameter into one you can use. The following code explains the same:

```
<%
strIP = GetSessionParam (g_cookie, "SourceIP")
SetSessionParamWithType g_cookie, "SourceIP_Policy", strIP, "Policy"
%>
```

The preceding code fetches the parameter `SourceIP`, which is normally an *internal* parameter, which is as such inaccessible to the endpoint policy, and injects it back with a different name and type. Now, you can refer to this as part of the endpoint policy!

Sending data to the backend server

Another nice trick you can pull with `PostPostValidate` is pushing data directly to a backend server in the HTTP Headers or the URL parameters. This could be useful, for example, if you want your backend server to be able to recognize that a request is coming from UAG, as opposed to a regular user that is accessing it. Another use could be if you want the app to be aware of the user even if there's no single-sign-on happening. For this, the following function is used:

```
SetSessionResourceParam g_cookie, <Application ID>, <Authorization
Key>, <Value>
```

For this to work, you also need to configure the relevant application. Let's say you are publishing your organization's ERP application and you want to give it the user's username in the request header. To do this, follow these steps:

1. Create the application and test it normally.

2. Open the **Application Properties** window, and obtain the **Application ID** from the **General** tab, as shown in the following screenshot:

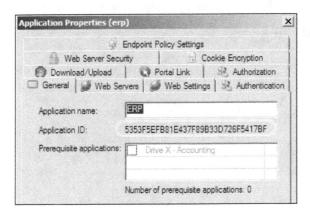

3. Choose a header value that is unique, and type it in the **Authorization key** in the application's **Web Settings** tab:

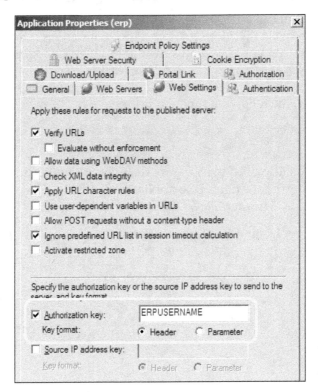

4. Create the following code in `PostPostValidate`:

```
<%
set colUserVec = getsessionuservec(g_cookie)
for each strUser in colUserVec.uservec
  strUserName = strUser.User
Next
SetSessionResourceParam g_cookie,
"5353F5EFB81E437F89B33D726F5417BF", "ERPUSERNAME, strUserName
%>
```

Now, when a user accesses the application, the logged on username will be sent as the value of the header `ERPUSERNAME`.

More ideas

The preceding info is just the tip of the iceberg, of course, as the things you can achieve by manipulating the session info are endless. The flexibility that ASP code provides you in pulling and pushing data from and to various resources, and the ability to manipulate the data using any VB command that ASP supports are a very powerful combination. If you really want to hone your knife, open the file `SessionMgr.inc` that we mentioned earlier, and inspect the various functions it offers to see if there are additional things that pick your interest. The file has about 50 functions, mostly related to the session info. In addition, the following are a few articles with further ideas:

*   The following article suggests a way to customize the Remote Desktop application in order to have a user connect automatically to his own desktop, as well as other related ideas:

    `http://technet.microsoft.com/en-us/library/ff607330.aspx`

*   The following article discusses redirecting users to alternative servers based on their information. The article was written for IAG, but the same code and principle applies to UAG as well:

    `http://technet.microsoft.com/en-us/library/dd278156.aspx`

*   The following blog post discusses the topic of Source IP address binding, and how to use it:

    `http://blogs.technet.com/b/edgeaccessblog/archive/2010/03/18/what-is-the-bind-the-source-ip-address-to-the-session-option.aspx`

- The following post describes configuring UAG to send request headers to published web applications using AppWrap:

  ```
  http://blogs.technet.com/b/edgeaccessblog/archive/2010/05/09/
  how-to-configure-uag-to-send-request-headers-to-published-web-
  applications.aspx
  ```

In addition to the preceding list, the topic is also frequently discussed in various UAG-related forums, and many of them include interesting ideas and informative code samples. Be sure to check these out!

Summary

In this chapter, we have discovered the power that manipulating the session data gives you, and discussed a few ideas of how to take advantage of that in making your UAG server and applications go above and beyond. In the next chapter, we will see how you can customize the client components to your advantage.

9
Customizing Endpoint Components

The endpoint components deployed by UAG to its clients (despite being almost invisible to the end user), pack quite a punch. They control the SSL Tunnel that the client uses for application tunneling; they wipe sensitive data off the client computer at the end of a session and can even reconfigure a computer's routing table to create the VPN connection of the network connector. Customizing these components is rare, but can help you provide a fantastic user experience.

In this chapter, we will explore the following topics:

- Adjusting the list of components pushed to clients by default
- Adding links to the portal for the client installation
- Customizing SSTP

Controlling component deployment

As you already know, as soon as a user types in the URL of a UAG application or portal, the first step is for UAG to detect if the user has the client components, and if not, install them. By default, UAG is configured to install only the basic set of components, which include the Client Component Manager, the Endpoint Session Cleanup component (also known as the Attachment Wiper), and the endpoint detection component. This means that if the portal hosts the **SSL-VPN tunneling application** (also known as the **network connector**), or some other application that requires SSL-VPN tunneling, launching these applications will require the installation of these additional components. This experience is somewhat unsavory, as the additional installation requires a browser restart. The solution is to customize the list of components installed by the portal automatically.

The list of components is controlled by the file `\von\InternalSite\InstallXml.asp`, which would be called in the following two situations:

- Upon entry to the portal, if the client components do not exist and need to be installed or upgraded
- When an application is launched from the portal

Upon portal entry, `InstallAndDetect.asp` calls `InstallXml.asp` in a `stage 1` mode, which instructs the component manager to install, by default, only the following components:

- Client Trace Utility
- Endpoint Detection
- Endpoint Session Cleanup
- Endpoint Session Cleanup Configuration
- Socket Forwarding Helper
- Endpoint Quarantine Enforcement Client
- SSL Network Tunneling_64

`SSL Network Tunneling_64` is not the actual tunneling component—it is just a helper component for it.

When an application is launched, the file `\Von\InternalSite\StartApp.asp` is called, and depending on the type of application, it may include the `stage=2` or `stage=4` parameter in the URL, which triggers an installation of additional components. Stage 2 mandates installation of SSL Application Tunneling. Stage 4 includes installation of Socket Forwarding.

`InstallXml.asp` is an ASP file that generates XML code that includes certain client components using the `response.write` command. For example, the Stage 2 piece looks similar to the following screenshot:

```
C:\temp\InstallXml.asp - metapad
File  Edit  Favourites  Options  Help

 if stage = 2 then
        Response.write "<Component Name=""""Client Trace Utility"""" ID=""""16"""" Install=""""1"""" />"
        Response.write "<Component Name=""""Socket Forwarding Helper"""" ID=""""9"""" Install=""""1"""" />"
        Response.write "<Component Name=""""SSL Application Tunneling"""" ID=""""1"""" Install=""""1"""" />"
        ' Always install SocketForwarder with SSL Application Tunneling when running on Vista...
        if lln_mode = 0 and uninstall_lln = "0" and remove_lln = "0" and force_lln then
                lln_mode = 1
        end if
 end if

DOS  INS  Line: 25/93  Col: 61
```

If we want to have UAG automatically install additional components, all we have to do is to add the ASP/XML code using a custom file. To do so, follow these steps:

1. In the `\Von\InternalSite\inc\CustomUpdate` folder, create a new file.

2. Name the file `InstallXml.inc`.

3. Within the file add the following code:

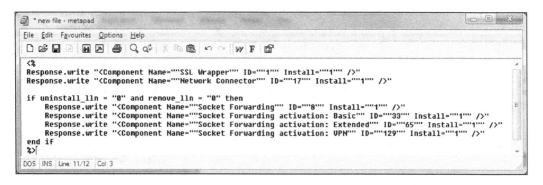

```
<%
Response.write "<Component Name=""SSL Wrapper"" ID=""1"" Install=""1"" />"
Response.write "<Component Name=""Network Connector"" ID=""17"" Install=""1"" />"

if uninstall_lln = "0" and remove_lln = "0" then
    Response.write "<Component Name=""Socket Forwarding"" ID=""8"" Install=""1"" />"
    Response.write "<Component Name=""Socket Forwarding activation: Basic"" ID=""33"" Install=""1"" />"
    Response.write "<Component Name=""Socket Forwarding activation: Extended"" ID=""65"" Install=""1"" />"
    Response.write "<Component Name=""Socket Forwarding activation: VPN"" ID=""129"" Install=""1"" />"
end if
%>
```

4. Save the file and activate the UAG configuration.

As you can probably guess, the second line instructs UAG to install the **SSL Application Tunneling** component (also known as the **SSL Wrapper**), and the third line installs the SSL Network Tunneling (also known as network connector). Lines 5 to 10 install the **Socket Forwarding** component, and also enable the three possible activation modes for the socket forwarder.

The socket forwarding activation modes are defined on the **Client Settings** tab of the applications you add to the UAG portal. In the **Basic** mode, the socket forwarder performs the forwarding only for interactive applications, and not for non-interactive ones (such as Windows services). In the **Extended** mode, traffic is forwarded for all applications, interactive or not. In the **VPN** mode, the socket forwarder component is always active, even before the SSL VPN tunnel is established.

Note that if you add the file this way, it will apply to all trunks configured on the server. You can set it, though, to apply to only a specific trunk by naming it using the standard UAG naming convention, where the file is named `<Trunk Name><1/0>InstallXml.inc`. For example, if your trunk is named UAGPortal, and it is an HTTP trunk, the target file should be named `UAGPortal0InstallXml.inc`.

Adding links to the portal for the client installation

As you probably know, in addition to the automatic installation of client components, UAG also comes with the client components as an installable **Microsoft Installer (MSI)** package. This allows a **pre-emptive** installation of the components on corporate computers, and can also sometimes help in case the online installation fails for some reason. When there is a need to provide the installation package to a user, a useful thing would be to provide a link to it so it could be downloaded directly from the UAG server, rather than having to use an e-mail attachment or some other mechanism.

UAG actually does part of that already. The installable packages are all located, in the `PortalHomePage` folder, by default:

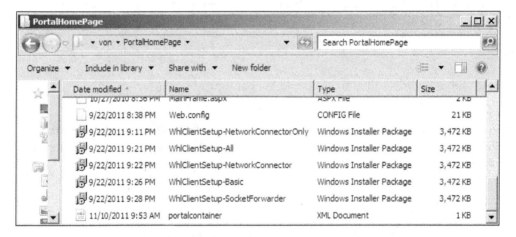

In fact, if you type in the URL for one of them in your browser, you would be able to download it directly. However, this requires that the client already has an authenticated UAG session, which may not be possible if he is having problems with the client components or if you want them installed before portal access.

The answer is to put the components in a place that is accessible without an authenticated session—in the `InternalSite` folder. This brings about the following three challenges:

- Access to URLs under `InternalSite` is restricted by default, so you need to place the files in a subfolder that is less restricted, or alternatively, create a URL-Set rule to allow access to it

- You need to make sure you place the file in a location that will not be removed with future UAG updates or service pack

- If you have an array, then you need to place the file in a place that is automatically synchronized between array members, or make sure you place it there manually on all members

Ultimately, the location itself is not that critical and where you put them will come down to personal choice. An obvious location, however, would be to create a folder named `On-DemandAgent` under `InternalSite`, as that folder already has a URL-Set rule permitting access to anything under it. The `OTP` folder under `InternalSite` is another location that is already accounted for by a predefined URL set. Alternatively, you could place it directly in `CustomUpdate` under `InternalSite`, and then simply create a URL-Set rule to allow it. Something along these lines:

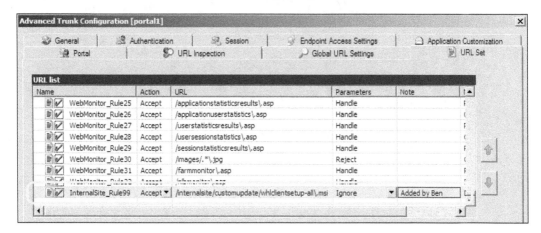

Note that we named the rule as number 99 intentionally. The rule set for UAG at this point in time has 60 rules for `InternalSite`, but future updates to UAG may add more, so we want to leave a decent amount of space to reduce the risk of our rule being overwritten in such a case.

With this in place, you could simply type the following URL into any browser:

```
https://<your_trunk>/internalsite/customupdate/whlclientsetup-all.msi
```

It should recognize the content type and offer to open or save the file. However, you probably want to take it to the next level, and place a link to it on the UAG portal itself. One place to do so would be the logon page itself. For this, you can customize the language file for the trunk, similar to what we discussed in *Chapter 2*, *Customizing UAG's Look and Feel*, and having one of the strings that are used in that page. Simply add the <A> HTML tag with the proper link within a CDATA element. Naturally, if the trunk's policy requires the endpoint components to have already been installed in order to access the login page, you might also put that link into the error page that would be displayed if the user does not have the components (that would be string ID 342 from /InternalSite/Languages/en-US.xml). For example, consider the following screenshot:

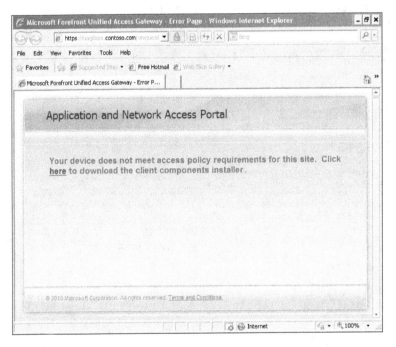

In addition to this, you can also customize the portal itself to display a link to the installer. Instructions for this are provided as part of the UAG technical documentation on TechNet at the following URL:

http://technet.microsoft.com/en-us/library/ee861162.aspx.

Customizing SSTP

SSTP is one of the strongest features UAG offers, making it a fully-fledged VPN solution that does not require any preconfiguration of client computers. The configuration options for SSTP, though, are somewhat limited. For example, SSTP does not allow for split tunneling, nor does it allow for the client to register itself in DNS, which is very useful if you need to establish connections to non-managed clients.

However with a simple customization, these two can be achieved, as well as additional fine-grained control of UAG's SSTP. The secret to achieving this is in the fact that UAG uses a **Phone Book (PBK)** file to hold the settings used by the client. With other VPN servers, the user creates a VPN connection entry, which is saved inside the user's PBK file, `rasphone.pbk`, typically located at `%AppData%\ Microsoft\network\connections\Pbk`. When UAG is in use, it creates a custom `SSTP.pbk` file, which is extracted from the file `WhlClntProxy.cab`, itself a part of the client components. This file is saved on the client, and when the user clicks on the **Remote Network Access** icon on the portal, it is launched in the background to establish the VPN connection.

If you were able to edit the default `SSTP.pbk`, you could control many settings yourself, but unfortunately, the CAB file used by the client components is digitally signed to prevent harmful tampering. However, the PBK file itself is a simple text file, which enables us to modify its content, if you know how!

We should note that the following technique is strongly related to the topics discussed in *Chapter 5, Creating Custom Application Templates*, but we decided it was more appropriate to discuss it here, as it is more pertinent to client-side customizations. If you have skipped *Chapter 5, Creating Custom Application Templates*, you should go back and read it through, as it lays the background.

The process we need to use here is based on customizing the VPN template used for the remote network access, and populating it with a VBScript that will modify the content of the `SSTP.pbk` file dynamically on the client before it is launched. We are actually creating a secondary application, which modifies the client components on the client, as opposed to changing the default SSTP application template. Once this application is in place, you will have to configure it as a prerequisite application for the SSTP application. The following is the code snippet:

```
<template name="SRScript" userrights="562" use-with-lsp="yes"
win="yes"><!--Windows-->
<port id="0" flags="1" ip2relay="169.1.1.169" remoteport="222"/>
<config-file flags="1" path="%Temp%\SSTPFix-%InternalAppID%.vbs"
use-with-lsp="yes"><![CDATA[
```

```
Const ForReading = 1
Const ForWriting = 2
strFileName = "%CommandLine%"
strOldText = "%CommandLineArguments%"
strNewText = "%CommandLineArguments2%"
Set objFSO = CreateObject("Scripting.FileSystemObject")
Set objFile = objFSO.OpenTextFile(strFileName, ForReading)
strText = objFile.ReadAll
objFile.Close
strNewText = Replace(strText, strOldText, strNewText)
Set objFile = objFSO.OpenTextFile(strFileName, ForWriting)
objFile.WriteLine strNewText
objFile.Close
]]>
</config-file>
<exec exe="cscript %temp%\SSTPFix-%InternalAppID%.vbs" flags="4"
param=""/><!--Windows-->
</template>
```

You can find the preceding code in the book's code folder, along with the accompanying custom `WizardDefaultParam.ini` code. The preceding code is a simple VBS function that takes three inputs—a source file, a search string, and a replace string. When it is integrated into the SSL VPN template this way, it will execute against the file named `C:\Program Files\Microsoft Forefront UAG\Endpoint Components\3.1.0\sstp.pbk`, and look for the text `IpPrioritizeRemote=1`, and replace it with `IpPrioritizeRemote=0`. This is comparable to editing the PBK file directly in the connection GUI and disabling the option **Use default gateway on remote network**, as shown in the following screenshot:

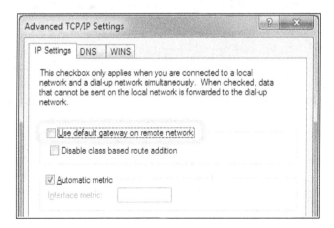

The option itself forces the VPN connection to *not* use the default gateway configured on the client computer, which enables **forced-tunneling** for the connection (also known as **non-split tunneling**). Using the same method, you could also change the text `IpDnsFlags=0` to `IpDnsFlags=1`, which would enable the option **Register this connection's addresses in DNS**, similar to checking this option in the GUI:

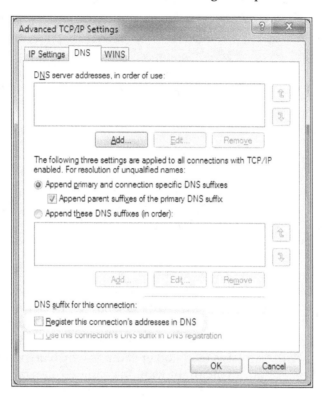

To make things clear, the preceding code needs to be implemented through a custom `SSLVPNTemplates.xml` file and must be structured within the standard `<config><templates version="3" use-lsp="1">..... </templates> </config>` format. This custom file then needs to be saved in `\von\Conf\CustomUpdate`, and corresponding `WizardDefaultParam.ini` file will need to be saved to the `\von\Conf\WizardDefaults\CustomUpdate` folder. Once added, you should close and reopen the management console for UAG to acknowledge the new application. Then head into the applications list and select our custom SSTP application.

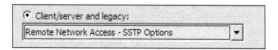

Step through the wizard until you get to the preceding dialog, which will allow you to specify the location of the pbk file and also the options you wish to search for and replace.

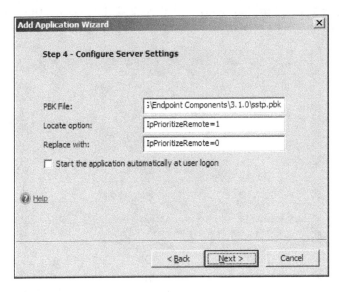

As noted earlier, this new application will have to be launched with or before the actual SSTP application, so configure it as a prerequisite application. You may also configure it to automatically launch with the login to the portal by enabling the option **Start the application automatically at user logon**. Naturally, the configuration will need to be activated afterwards and doing this will affect all clients. The UAG PBK file contains many other settings which are worth looking into, as you might find other things you might want to change. To extract the file and inspect it, simply go to \von\InternalSite\Win32\ActiveX and double-click the file WhlClntProxy.cab. In it, find SSTP.pbk and copy it somewhere, and then open it with a text editor of your choice, such as notepad:

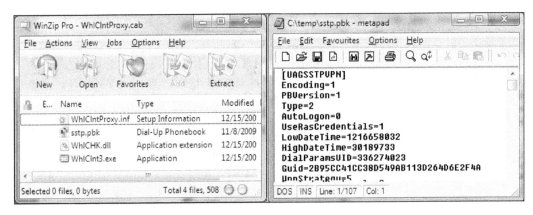

Summary

In this chapter, we discussed some of the things you can do to enhance the experience on UAG clients with customizations. As you can see, there are not that many options there, but those that do exist could be vital to many organizations. In the next chapter, we will discuss a few remaining tidbits, as well as some more general customization thoughts and ideas. Don't go away, we're not done yet!

10

Additional Customizations

We have covered many types and variants of customizations in this book, but some do not really fit into a particular category, and this is what this chapter is about. Some of these may not even seem like a customization, but they are extremely important nonetheless. In this chapter, we will look at the following topics:

- Customizations to the UAG console
- Remote management and monitoring of UAG
- Additional files you can customize
- Extending file access with DFS shares
- Skipping cookie signing
- Custom logouts

Customizations to the UAG console

You probably noticed this already in your endeavors with UAG—the activation process completes and the console notifies you with the pop-up, but the changes you made don't appear to have taken effect. In fact, they always do take effect, but only a few minutes after the pop-up is shown. What actually happens is that the activation itself finishes, but the TMG side of the house remains busy synchronizing data with TMG storage, and that can take an additional 2 to 3 minutes. The more intricate the configuration the longer this takes, and if you don't wait those extra minutes, you'll probably notice that changes have not taken effect, but at the same time you will not be able to reactivate until the sync has completed. Those making the odd change from time to time can simply activate and wait a few minutes, but when faced with countless activations, a much better option is to enable informational messages.

This configures UAG to display more detailed information about what it is doing during this process and the output is shown at the bottom part of the UI. To turn that on, follow these steps:

1. Open the UAG console.

2. Open the **Messages** menu and click **Filter Messages**.

3. Check the left **informational messages** option.

4. Click **OK**.

From now on, when you activate the configuration, you will see a lot of info displayed, and it will eventually reach **Waiting for TMG storage to synchronize**, and finally **activation completed successfully**. Only then will your activation be truly complete.

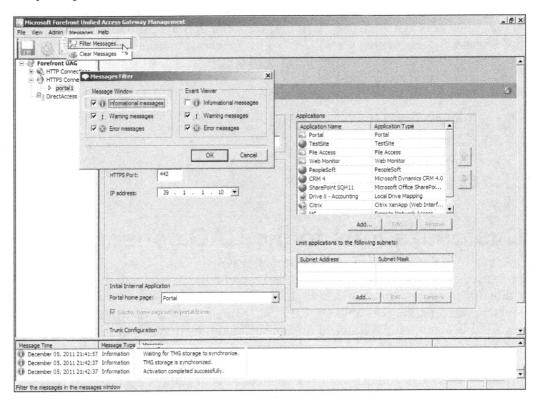

A final note on this is that if you are running an array of UAG servers, don't expect the message bar to show you what's going on with other array members. For that, you will have to use the **Activation Monitor**, which you can find in the UAG folder on your start menu.

Remote management and monitoring of UAG

Most administrators use remote desktop to take control of their UAG server rather than working on the server locally. However, unless you installed your server using remote desktop, you may find that you are unable to connect to it. This is not a bug, but an out-of-the-box security mechanism that's intentionally there to protect UAG from unauthorized access. Remote access to UAG is then only permitted from sources that have been explicitly listed in TMG. So as an administrator, you would need to add your required sources to the predefined remote management object. To do so, the following steps are to be carried out:

1. Open the TMG console.
2. Click on **Firewall Policy**.
3. On the right-hand side of the screen, go to **Toolbox**.
4. Expand **Network Objects**.
5. Expand **Computer Sets**.
6. Double-click on **Remote Management Computers**.

It's probably worth mentioning that modifying the TMG configuration directly is normally *not supported*, but the preceding procedure is one rare exception to the *don't touch TMG* rule where remote access is a must. The reality is that most administrators are tempted to use TMG to its full potential, and with all of its features it's difficult not to. Just keep in mind that not only is this *not supported*, but adding user-defined TMG rules may invariably conflict with the configurations that UAG is responsible for managing.

Add to that group any computer, address range, or subnet you wish to grant access from, as shown in the following screenshot:

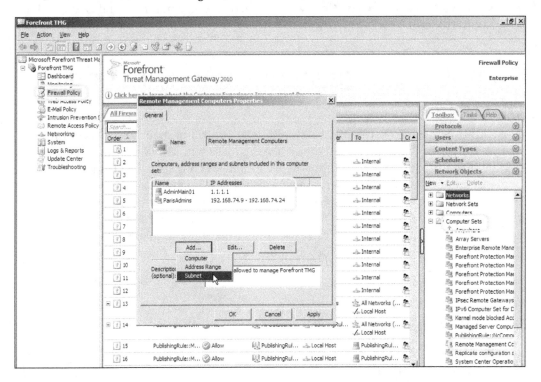

As with the Remote Access rule, other configurations may go unnoticed, but in some cases it can also introduce enough of a conflict to prevent UAG from successfully activating. Another thing that's worth bearing in mind is that it's also tempting to add the entire subnet for your corporate network, but this does nothing for security and presents unnecessary risk. A potential hacker would still need to be a domain admin (or local admin) to cause real damage to UAG, but we're sure that this is something you wouldn't want to encourage, given that your UAG links your internal network to the public Internet...right?

Remote management software

Many organizations prefer to use third-party solutions to manage their servers, and a common requirement in almost every case is that the management server remains in dialog with an agent running on the managed device. With this, you might run into issues as TMG will block such requests. As before, adjusting the TMG configuration manually is not supported, but don't despair, as there is a way. What you want is to convince TMG to allow data through, and a supported way of doing this is simple—use a Client/Server application template. These templates include a configuration for a server or servers, and port or ports, and as part of that, UAG will configure TMG to allow that traffic. To do so, follow these steps:

1. Open the UAG console and add a new application.

2. From the **Client/Server and legacy** application template group, select **Generic Client Application** if the communication used is with one target server and using one TCP/IP port. Select **Generic Client Application (Multiple Servers)** if you want to allow access to many servers, or to one server using multiple ports.

3. Give the application a name to your liking.

4. In the **Server Settings** page, specify the details. If you need to specify multiple ports in the **Generic Client Application (Multiple Servers)** application, do so with a comma between numbers. You can also use a range like **20-40**.

5. In the **Portal Link** page, disable the option **Add a portal and toolbar link**, as your users will not be using this application.

6. Finish the wizard and activate the configuration.

Monitoring UAG health by SIEM software or a load balancer

Infrastructures are becoming more complex by the day and the requirements for high availability and **Disaster Recovery (DR)** are forcing corporations into moving their systems into secure data facilities which most of the time are completely unmanned. In this scenario, we're often left not knowing if things are running smoothly until it's too late, so a fairly common approach to avoid high impact is to remotely keep an eye on the server's, and ultimately UAG's, health.

Health monitoring could also be required if you have an array of UAG servers that were front ended by an external load balancer. In this arrangement, a load balancer would need to persistently monitor the status and availability of its UAG targets in order to validate their availability and whether all of them are accepting connections or not responding. Another common scenario is if your organization uses a **Security Information Event Monitoring** (**SIEM**, also known as **SIM** or **SEM**) to keep track of servers and key devices and in turn notifying the operations teams, if one goes down.

Most of these solutions offer some kind of connectivity-checking capabilities, and you may have instinctively already set it to monitor UAG. However, there's a very good chance that you have done so incorrectly. If so, it's likely that UAG will perceive the monitoring software's connections as user sessions, and will try to keep track of them. This isn't ideal, as the frequent checks waste valuable UAG server resources, and worse case may even trip a flood-mitigation alert in TMG, which will cause it to block connections from the monitoring component completely. Naturally, this will also cause the UAG activity log to inflate, which will in turn make it hard or impossible for you to query the logs for usage data. They will either return a huge number of irrelevant events, or the log will be so large that it will cause a memory exception in the log parser.

> TMG, being an enterprise-class firewall, monitors incoming traffic, and a repeating pattern may be considered a flood attack. When TMG interprets traffic as such, it may block the traffic, causing your monitoring device to think the server is not responding. This, of course, is not very desirable. For more information on flood mitigation in TMG, visit the following URL:
>
> `http://technet.microsoft.com/en-us/library/dd441028.aspx`.

The right way to do it is to set the monitoring component to check UAG's pulse in a way that will not appear as a connecting user. For this, the following steps are to be carried out:

1. Create a text file named `test.vbs.sig`.

2. Put some unique string in the file, which would not exist in another UAG page (the name of your favorite character from Star Trek, perhaps?).

3. Place the file in `\von\internalsite\CustomUpdate\`.

4. Configure your load balancer to make a request for `https://<Your portal>/internalsite/customupdate/test.vbs.sig` to perform its monitoring.

5. Activate the configuration.

6. Set the load balancer to see the result as **positive** or **alive**, if the content of the request matches the string you have used in step 2.

The reason for using a file with this extension (`.vbs.sig`) is that UAG's default URL Set will allow access to that file without requiring you to manually edit the URL Set.

In addition, carefully consider the frequency of the polling, as a setting that is too frequent could still trigger the flood mitigation in TMG. Please review the article listed previously, and configure the polling frequency accordingly.

Additional files you can customize

In the various chapters, we have referred to many files you can or cannot customize, while also having discussed the special `CustomUpdate` folders. You may have already noticed that there are close to 50 different folders out there, but that doesn't mean you can just drop any file in there and it will be eaten up by UAG. In fact, only certain files of the default file sets are *supported* for customization. This doesn't mean that Microsoft Customer Support will support anything you change to those files that are supported, just that UAG has the existing code to be able to parse those files. You might find yourself wondering, then, which files are actually customizable and which aren't. The answer to this is that the files that are supported get called by a special function named `include Application`. You can see that function in several files. For example, here it is in `\Von\InternalSite\Login.inc`:

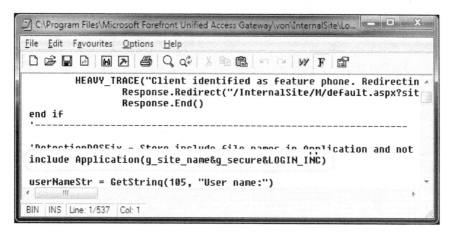

This format tells UAG to look for a file named after the trunk (g_site_name), and the secure flag of 0 or 1, and then the suffix, set in the constant LOGIN_INC. That constant is set in another file, \Von\InternalSite\inc\IncludeFiles.inc, alongside the constant files names for many other such files. For example:

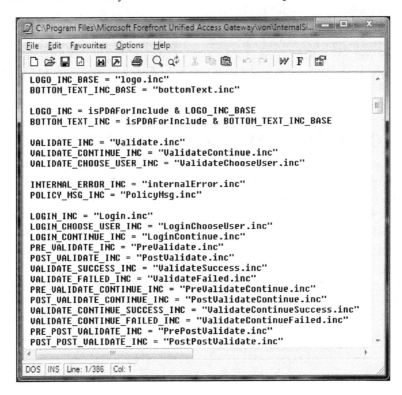

```
LOGO_INC_BASE = "logo.inc"
BOTTOM_TEXT_INC_BASE = "bottomText.inc"

LOGO_INC = isPDAForInclude & LOGO_INC_BASE
BOTTOM_TEXT_INC = isPDAForInclude & BOTTOM_TEXT_INC_BASE

VALIDATE_INC = "Validate.inc"
VALIDATE_CONTINUE_INC = "ValidateContinue.inc"
VALIDATE_CHOOSE_USER_INC = "ValidateChooseUser.inc"

INTERNAL_ERROR_INC = "internalError.inc"
POLICY_MSG_INC = "PolicyMsg.inc"

LOGIN_INC = "Login.inc"
LOGIN_CHOOSE_USER_INC = "LoginChooseUser.inc"
LOGIN_CONTINUE_INC = "LoginContinue.inc"
PRE_VALIDATE_INC = "PreValidate.inc"
POST_VALIDATE_INC = "PostValidate.inc"
VALIDATE_SUCCESS_INC = "ValidateSuccess.inc"
VALIDATE_FAILED_INC = "ValidateFailed.inc"
PRE_VALIDATE_CONTINUE_INC = "PreValidateContinue.inc"
POST_VALIDATE_CONTINUE_INC = "PostValidateContinue.inc"
VALIDATE_CONTINUE_SUCCESS_INC = "ValidateContinueSuccess.inc"
VALIDATE_CONTINUE_FAILED_INC = "ValidateContinueFailed.inc"
PRE_POST_VALIDATE_INC = "PrePostValidate.inc"
POST_POST_VALIDATE_INC = "PostPostValidate.inc"
```

As you can see in the preceding screenshot, this refers to files we dealt with before, such as Logo.inc and PostPostValidate.inc. This is also where you can find the answer regarding which files you can customize—if a filename is referred to here, it means UAG has the Include Application function somewhere to call it, meaning that if you put it in CustomUpdate, it will be included and used. This doesn't mean that the customization will be simple. Take logo.inc, for example—the original file has the following code in it:

```
C:\Program Files\Microsoft Forefront Unified Access Gateway\von\InternalSite\inc\logo.inc - metapad

File  Edit  Favourites  Options  Help

<%'include file for title
' xxxxxxxxxxxxxxxxxxxxxxx DO NOT EDIT THIS FILE xxxxxxxxxxxxxxxxxxxxxxxxxx
' A.O.detectionDOSFix - Store include file names in Application and not in Session.
if Application(g_site_name&g_secure&LOGO_INC) <> FILE_NOT_EXIST then
        include Application(g_site_name&g_secure&LOGO_INC)
else%>
<tr>
        <td class="headerTop" colspan="3">
                <table width="100%" border="0" cellspacing="0" cellpadding="0">
                        <tr>
                                <td class="header1"><%=GetString(2, "Application and Network Access
Portal")%></td>
                        </tr>
                </table>
        </td>
</tr>
<tr>
        <td class="headertext" colspan="3"></td>
</tr>
<%end if%>

DOS  INS  Line: 1/21  Col: 1
```

If you try to copy the file and change the HTML alone, it would cause UAG to produce a 500 error because the code is recursive. For such a trick to work properly, you will need to remove the `if/then/else/end if` structure and leave only the HTML. You should be able to put your own ASP code in there, if needed, of course, but make sure that the `include application` function is removed so as to not cause a conflict.

> When going through UAG's code, you might find yourself in need of finding where a certain function or command appears. A useful command for this is the **FINDSTR**, which you can use in a command prompt. Typically, you would use it with the `/I` and `/S` options to tell the search to not be case-sensitive and search subfolders. For example:
>
> Findstr /I /S /c:"include application" *.asp
>
> This will show each of the 19 files that have this function in them.

In addition to these files, some other files can also be customized. For example, we have already discussed in *Chapter 2, Customizing UAG's Look and Feel,* how you can drop icon images files into `CustomUpdate` and UAG will use them automatically. You can do the same with many other files, but unfortunately, there's no list of these or any concrete way of telling which would work and which wouldn't other than by trial-and-error.

It's very important to keep in mind, though, that customizing UAG's code files is tricky and risky. While many of them will be called and processed if put into `CustomUpdate`, their code is not always designed to work correctly in this situation, which could result in an error such as the 500 error we mentioned previously. Furthermore, these files often change as part of UAG updates and service packs, and so a newer file may refer to functions or variables your custom file does not have, also leading to various possible issues. In other words, we recommend you focus your attention on customizing the supported INC files, and look into others only if no other choice exists. If you do have no choice, experiment to see if the file you want to touch can be customized or not (copying it into `CustomUpdate` and adding some line of text or output-generating command would be a reasonable way to check) and if so, tread carefully and perform a lot of testing.

Extending File Access with DFS shares

The File Access application built into UAG has fantastic capabilities, but also some limitations. One of these is lack of support for DFS shares. By this we mean that you will not even see DFS shares as they just do not appear. Technically, the application can connect to DFS shares, but the admin tool is unable to enumerate them, so you cannot add them. There is, however, a custom way of forcing File Access to use them. This entails editing the XML file which contains the list of servers and shares you selected with the admin tool.

All changes made in the File Access UI are written to this file in real time, so don't be alarmed if you see the contents change when the file is opened in an editor.

The process of editing the file is as follows:

1. Navigate to your UAG install directory, under `\von\fileaccess`.
2. Open the UAG management console.
3. Backup the `ShareAccesscfg.xml` file and then using a text editing tool, open the original.
4. Within the `<Servers>` section, add an item for your domain using the following format:

   ```
   <server name="<Your Domain>\<Your DFS namespace>" marked="1"
   provider="MS" />
   ```

5. Within the `<Shares>` section, add an item for each DFS share using the following format:

   ```
   <share name="<Your Domain>\<Your DFS Namespace>\<DFS Share Name>"
   marked="1" provider="MS" />
   ```

6. Save the file.

7. Activate the UAG configuration.

One thing you might consider doing before saving and activating is to validate the XML syntax. Other than using your own eyes for this, a tool such as the one found at the URL `http://validator.w3.org/` can help make things a little easier.

You should be aware that changes made to this file can be overwritten by UAG, as the TMG storage has a copy of the previous configuration (even if it is blank). In this case, you would still be able to make your required changes, but they will not remain permanent as any of the following four actions will simply overwrite the contents of the file with whatever UAG finds in the TMG storage for File Access:

- Activating or closing and reopening the management UI
- Clicking **Reload Configuration** from the **File** menu in the UAG management UI
- Restarting the UAG Configuration Manager service
- Restarting the UAG server

The reason for this is that UAG holds its running configuration in several locations, such as the server's memory and the TMG storage, in addition to its file-level structure, so the trick to work around this and make your changes permanent is to do the following:

1. Close the UAG management console.

2. Set the `IgnoreTMGStore` registry to entry to `1` as per the following KB article:

   `http://technet.microsoft.com/en-us/library/ee809087.aspx`.

3. Make your changes to the `ShareAccesscfg.xml` file.

4. Restart the Microsoft Forefront UAG Configuration Manager service.

5. Launch the UAG management console.

6. Restore the `IgnoreTMGStore` registry entry to `0`.

7. Activate the UAG configuration.

The preceding sequence should force a purge of all UAG configuration data while allowing your changes to be written back to TMG storage. Once complete, you must avoid ever making any further changes in the UAG File Access UI, as this will overwrite all of your good work.

In the following screenshot we have added line breaks and formatting to the XML. Your own file would be one continuous line. You may format it for convenience, though it is not required:

Another thing to note about this is that the same technique can be used to configure UAG to provide access to shares manually, in case the share enumeration that the admin tool performs cannot be used. This may be the case, for example, if the domain or network are not configured to allow the share enumeration process, or if the amount of servers and shares is very large and takes the tool too long to complete.

Skipping cookie signing

As you probably know, in addition to signing URLs in the contents of pages delivered to the client, UAG also performs a similar process with cookies sent by the server. The reason is the same – to be able to match the cookies to the application the user is using and forwarding them to the correct backend server, and only it. However, occasionally you might find yourself needing to avoid that process. Typically, this would be required for applications that have client-side handling code, which would not be able to *see* these cookies, as their name is different from what the application would be expecting.

One specific example of this is PeopleSoft, which uses multiple cookies, and quite a lot of client-side code to handle them. When publishing this application with the standard template, UAG will sign all the cookies, and that will cause the client-side code to think the user's session with the PeopleSoft server has expired, and send him/her to an error page:

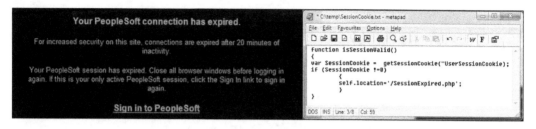

This type of situation is not always simple to resolve, as it would typically require some level of reverse-engineering of the application's code, to find out what it is expecting and why it is falsely thinking the session has expired. In this case, this is triggered by a JavaScript function similar to the above, on the right (the preceding code is *not* PeopleSoft's copyright-protected code, of course). The function looks for a cookie by name, and when it fails to find it, redirects to the error page. In such a case, the solution is to craft a custom SRA file (see *Chapter 4*, *The Application Wrapper and SRA*, if you need to refresh your memory on those) which will instruct UAG to not sign the cookie. There is no specific command to avoid the signing, but configuring UAG to remove the cookie's path and domain will trigger this behavior.

The following is a sample SRA file to handle two of the PeopleSoft cookies:

```
C:\temp\WhlFiltSecureRemote_HTTPS.xml - metapad

File  Edit  Favourites  Options  Help

<WHLFILTSECUREREMOTE ver="2.2">
        <COOKIES_HANDLING>
                <APPLICATION>
                        <APPLICATION_TYPE>PeopleSoft</APPLICATION_TYPE>
                        <URL>.*</URL>
                        <Set-Cookie>
                                <NAME>PS_LOGINLIST</NAME>
                                <Domain remove="true">WHL_SERVER_NAME</Domain>
                                <Path remove="true"></Path>
                        </Set-Cookie>
                </APPLICATION>
                <SERVER>
                        <SERVER_NAME mask="">PSSRV01</SERVER_NAME>
                        <Set-Cookie>
                                <NAME>PS_TOKENEXPIRE</NAME>
                                <Domain remove="true">WHL_SERVER_NAME</Domain>
                                <Path remove="true"></Path>
                        </Set-Cookie>
                </SERVER>
        </COOKIES_HANDLING>
</WHLFILTSECUREREMOTE>

DOS  INS  Line: 18/22  Col: 37
```

The preceding sample shows the two common schemes—find the cookies by application type and URL, and find the cookies by server name. We should point out that the preceding code is not a complete solution to problem you may face with publishing PeopleSoft. Different versions of it require different changes, in addition to using the correct server name or application URLs.

Custom logouts

Customizing the logout pages is a confusing case of mixed simplicity and complexity. On one hand, it's really simple to adjust the path in the UAG's user interface:

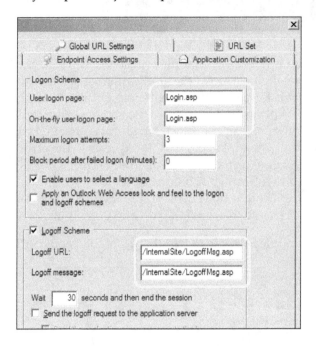

However, on the other hand this simplicity also hides a few dangerous curve balls. The problem is in the fact that the login and logout code is extremely important, and a code bug in there may lead to horrible results that can be hard to predict or trace. For example, during logout, UAG clears some important cookies. If you have customized the logout page in a way that circumvents the cookie clearing code, the cookies left behind may confuse UAG's user- and session-tracking mechanisms and lead to various errors and strange behavior.

Another thing that handles cookies is the **Endpoint Cleanup** component, which is a part of UAG's endpoint components. Some customers choose to disable the endpoint components without realizing that this could leave the client computer with cookies that may contain sensitive data. This is not only a security risk, but also a session management risk. In such a situation, if the user connects to a published app with old cookies in place, it could confuse the application as it tries to figure out if the user does already have a session or not.

An additional pain point comes from the fact that Microsoft does change UAG's code as part of updates and service packs of the product, and these changes may include changes to the Login or Logoff pages, and changes to other code that depend on it. In such a situation, UAG will not be able to update your custom file, and that could lead to a problem. For example, when UAG SP1 came out in early 2011, many customers with custom Login pages discovered their customization was no longer compatible with other code, causing various errors. This is typically not very hard to fix—you just need to apply whatever customizations were added to the original `login.asp` file, to the new `login.asp` file. However, some companies had their customization done by a third-party consultant, and were not even aware of it and unsure how to resolve the situation.

To customize these pages, the following regular process applies:

1. Copy the original file into `\Von\InternalSite\CustomUpdate`.
2. Edit the file, and make changes to it as needed.
3. Adjust the path in **Advanced Trunk Configuration** to match the new file (note that the login page path should not start with a slash).

In case you are wondering there's no need to adjust the rule set, as the default rules are already prepared for a custom Login and Logoff (InternalSite rules 1 and 12):

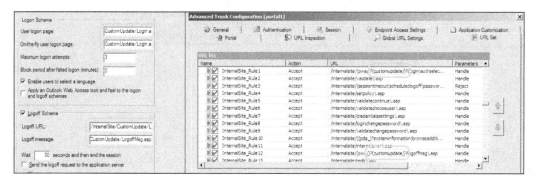

If you do need to customize these pages, this is not much different than customizing any ASP page, but the following are some things to keep in mind:

- Prefer to adjust the contents by changing the strings in the language files, as described in *Chapter 2, Customizing UAG's look and feel*.

- If customizing, `Login.asp` is needed. See if you can achieve your goal by using a custom `login.inc` instead of touching the ASP itself (`\von\InternalSite\inc\CustomUpdate\login.inc`).

- Base your custom files on the default files, rather than create them from scratch, and make every possible effort to avoid removing any of the original UAG code from your custom file, unless you know very well what it does and have a good reason to believe it will do no harm.

- Perform thorough testing of your code, deeper than any other testing you regularly do. If you can employ a tester to help, even better!

If you are customizing `Logoffmsg.asp`, pay close attention to the multiple `include file` commands. The file has seven of those, and they refer to a specific file location which becomes invalid if you run the file from another folder. To get around this, change the command from `Include File` to `Include Virtual`, and the path from `inc/` to `InternalSite/inc/`.

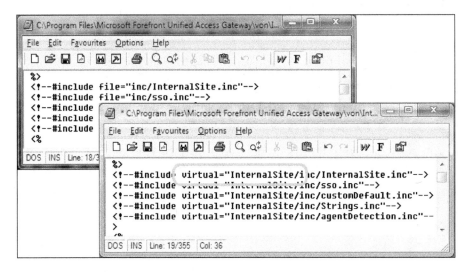

Another important thing to know about customizing the logoff process is the difference between **Logoff URL** and **Logoff Message**. The latter is the file that UAG will call when the user clicks on the **Logoff** button (the file you would be customizing!), but the former is a URL pattern that will trigger UAG's logoff process. This is useful for situations where you are publishing an application that has its own **Logoff** button. In such a situation, you might prefer that the application's button will trigger a logoff from the UAG portal rather than logoff just the application while leaving the UAG session active. UAG actually does this for you when publishing certain applications, such as SharePoint or OWA. This is somewhat related to stuff we discussed briefly in *Chapter 4*, *The Application Wrapper and SRA*. Back then, we saw how UAG hides OWA's **Logoff** button so that the user will use the UAG **Logoff** button instead of OWA's.

However, UAG has another piece of AppWrap which, when OWA is used without the portal frame replaces the regular OWA logoff code with code to trigger the UAG's logoff page (there are several of these, for the various OWA versions and variations—one such example is in lines 504 to 511 in the default AppWrap file).

For example, let's say you are publishing a PeopleSoft server. It would have a **Sign Out** button, which triggers a URL similar to `/psp/EMPLOYEE/HR/?cmd=logout`, as we can see in the following source code. If you want UAG to logoff the session when the user clicks on that button, configure the **Logoff URL** in UAG to the string `cmd=logout` URL, and that's it!

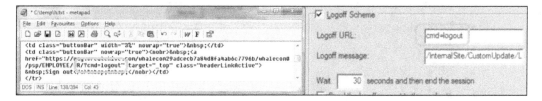

Naturally, this needs to be well researched by analyzing the application, as it could be a double-edged sword. If, for example, PeopleSoft has some other URL that is part of the normal operation of the app, but contains that string, it will be an epic fail, as executing that operation will log the user off unintentionally. Tread carefully!

Summary

This is it! Having read through this entire book, you should have a solid understanding of UAG's customization framework, and you may be able to fully grasp the immense power customization gives you. You may also be seeing how flexible UAG is with its ability to take your own code and configuration to a much more extensive degree than most other software products out there.

Forty years ago, when the market for personal computers boomed, tweaking and customizing was what drew some of the most amazing innovators into this field. With UAG, this is exactly the kind of fun you can have, developing your own creative solutions and new ways to accomplish your goals. It may be tricky walking the path that is supported, but once having gotten used to that, we are sure you will achieve great things!

Before signing off, we would like to acknowledge some people whose great work and research with UAG has contributed to some of the creative thoughts and ideas expressed in this book, or to the world of UAG customization:

- Alexandre Giraud
- Assaf Ronen
- Billy Price
- Bryan Goldstein
- Chris Cooper
- Dan Herzog
- Dan Watson
- Dennis Lee
- Doc Miller
- Dominik Zemp
- Dror Melovany
- Dror Zelber
- Eli Tovbeyn
- Eyal Peri
- Faisal Hussain
- Frederic Esnouf
- Ian Parramore
- Idan Plotnik
- Jan Tietze
- Jason Jones
- Jeff Lilleskare
- John Neystadt
- John Redding
- Masoud Hoghooghi
- Meir Mendelovich
- Michel Biton
- Mike Havens
- Mohit Saxena
- Ophir Polotsky
- Ori Yosefi
- Phil Bevan
- Pradeep Bethi
- Ran Dolev
- Renan Gutman
- Renato Menezes
- Richard Barker
- Richard Hicks
- Ron Gilad
- Tarun Sachdeva
- Thomas Detzner
- Tom Shinder
- Tom Sullivan
- Uri Arjitecter
- Uri Lichtenfeld
- Yan Mintz
- Yassine Khelifi

Index

certificate authentication
  about 91
  advantages 93
  concepts 92
  troubleshooting 103-106
Certificate Authority. *See* CA
cert.inc file 99
Certutil 94
Character Data. *See* CDATA
client installation
  links, adding to portal 136, 137
clients
  portal, selecting 39-41
CMD-Shell commands 78
CN 100
code
  debugging 114, 115
  testing 114, 115
COM object 44, 113
computer certificates 95
content alteration 58
cookie signing
  skipping 156-158
Create as script option 51
Cryptographic Service Provider. *See* CSP-
    API
cryptographic store
  about 94
  computer store 94
  current user store 94
  services store 94
crypto store. *See* cryptographic store
CSCRIPT 114
CSP API 95
CSS 24
Current User container 95
CustomUpdate 22, 23, 153
CustomUpdate scheme 40

D

data
  putting, into session 125-127
  sending, to backend server 129-131
Data Change function 66
DATA_CHANGE function 64
DB connection 112

DebugEcho
  statement 53
DefaultSchema setting 85
detection
  editing 40
  expression 40
detection script
  about 45
  client component detection component ,
      version checking 45
  custom detection script, creating 48
  custom detection script, placing 48
  custom detection script, tips 49
  custom detection script, with endpoint poli-
      cies 49-52
  debugging 53, 54
  DNS Suffix, checking 46
  domain membership, checking 46
  Endpoint Session Cleanup component, ver-
      sion checking 45
  environment variables, retrieving 46
  file existence, checking 46
  local user's access level, checking 46
  modification date, checking 46
  operating system version, checking for 47
  registry key, reading 46
  Service Pack level, checking 46
  SSL-VPN Tunneling component, version
      checking 46
  troubleshooting 53, 54
  UAG hostname. value checking 46
  Whale.AttachmentWiperVersion method
      45
  Whale COM object 45
  Whale.DetectorVersion method 45
  Whale.ExternalHost method 46
  Whale.FileSystem.DateLastModified
      method 46
  Whale.FileSystem.Exist method 46
  Whale.FileSystem.ProductVersion method
      46
  Whale.Processes.Filter method 46
  Whale.Registry.RegRead method 46
  Whale.ShowDebugMessages method 46
  Whale.SSLVPNVersion method 46
  Whale.System.ExpandEnvironmentStr
      method 46

---

response.write command 134
Running value 124

S

sAMAccountName 97
SAM-Account-Name. *See*
    sAMAccountName
SAN 97
SAR section 66
sDomain variable 113
SEARCH tag 66
secure channel 93
Secure Remote Access. *See* SRA
security center 44
Security Information Event Monitoring.
    See SIEM
SEM. *See* SIEM
Server-Side Include. *See* SSI
Service Pack level 46
Service Principal Name. *See* SPN
SetSessionParamWithType function 127
ShortDesc 85
SIEM 150
sign_abs_path option 70
Sign out button 58, 60, 63
SIM. *See* SIEM
Simple Relay mode 87
Single Sign On. *See* SSO
Smartcard Logon 93-95
Smartcard User 93-95
Smartcard User certificate 95
Socket Forwarding component 135
soft certificate 96
SPN 102
SQL database 111, 112
SQL Select query 111
SRA
    about 58
    configuration file 69
    syntax 68
SRA configuration files
    and AppWrap 59
SRA engine
    and AppWrap, working 60-62
SSI 24

SSL Application Tunneling component. *See*
    SSL Wrapper
SSL Network Tunneling_64 134
SSLVpnTemplate parameter 85
SSL-VPN templates
    about 74, 75
    configuration 85, 86
    settings 85, 86
    SSLVPNTemplates.xml template, structure
        87
    storage 73
SSL-VPN tunneling application 133
SSL Wrapper 135
SSO 84, 102
SSTP
    customizing 139, 140
strong authentication 93
Subject Alternative Name. *See* SAN
SubjectEMAIL field 101
SystemFileObject COM object 124

T

TechNet
    URL 34, 138
templates
    creating 76
    creating, steps 76, 77
    customizing 77, 78
    parameters 79
    WizardDefault file 79-82
Terminal Services (TS) 47, 82
text
    changing 36
TGS 105
The Application Wrapper. *See* AppWrap
Ticket Granting Service. *See* TGS
TMG 105, 150
TMG Storage 49
TRACE function 26
trace.inc, code file 26

U

UA COM object
    code, integrating 123

Thank you for buying
Mastering Microsoft Forefront
UAG 2010 Customization

About Packt Publishing

Packt, pronounced 'packed', published its first book "Mastering phpMyAdmin for Effective MySQL Management" in April 2004 and subsequently continued to specialize in publishing highly focused books on specific technologies and solutions.

Our books and publications share the experiences of your fellow IT professionals in adapting and customizing today's systems, applications, and frameworks. Our solution based books give you the knowledge and power to customize the software and technologies you're using to get the job done. Packt books are more specific and less general than the IT books you have seen in the past. Our unique business model allows us to bring you more focused information, giving you more of what you need to know, and less of what you don't.

Packt is a modern, yet unique publishing company, which focuses on producing quality, cutting-edge books for communities of developers, administrators, and newbies alike. For more information, please visit our website: www.packtpub.com.

About Packt Enterprise

In 2010, Packt launched two new brands, Packt Enterprise and Packt Open Source, in order to continue its focus on specialization. This book is part of the Packt Enterprise brand, home to books published on enterprise software – software created by major vendors, including (but not limited to) IBM, Microsoft and Oracle, often for use in other corporations. Its titles will offer information relevant to a range of users of this software, including administrators, developers, architects, and end users.

Writing for Packt

We welcome all inquiries from people who are interested in authoring. Book proposals should be sent to author@packtpub.com. If your book idea is still at an early stage and you would like to discuss it first before writing a formal book proposal, contact us; one of our commissioning editors will get in touch with you.

We're not just looking for published authors; if you have strong technical skills but no writing experience, our experienced editors can help you develop a writing career, or simply get some additional reward for your expertise.

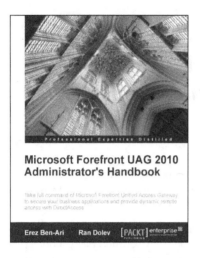

Microsoft Forefront UAG 2010 Administrator's Handbook

ISBN: 978-1-84968-162-9   Paperback: 484 pages

Take full command of Microsoft ForeFront Unified Access Gateway to secure your business application and provide dynamic remote access with DirectAccess

1. Maximize your business results by fully understanding how to plan your UAG integration

2. Consistently be ahead of the game by taking control of your server with backup and advanced monitoring

3. An essential tutorial for new users and a great resource for veterans

Microsoft Dynamics CRM 2011 Reporting and Business Intelligence

ISBN: 978-1-84968-230-5   Paperback: 300 pages

Create better, smarter, professional reports in Dynamics CRM 2011

1. Create easily understood, professional, and powerful reports from disordered, scattered data

2. Covers exciting new reporting features in Dynamics CRM 2011 such as inline data visualization and presentation, charts, dashboards, fetchxml query based reports, BIDS extension for SQL SRS based reports, and more

Please check **www.PacktPub.com** for information on our titles

Microsoft Dynamics CRM 2011: Dashboards Cookbook

ISBN: 978-1-84968-440-8   Paperback: 266 pages

Over 50 simple but incredibly effective recipes for creating, customizing and interacting with rich dashboards and charts to make the most of your Microsoft Dynamics CRM data with this book and ebook

1. Take advantage of all of the latest Dynamics CRM dashboard features for visualizing your most important data at a glance.

2. Understand how iFrames, chart customizations, advanced WebResources and more can improve your dashboards in Dynamics CRM by using this book and eBook.

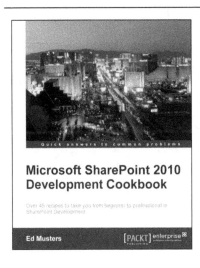

Microsoft SharePoint 2010 development cookbook

ISBN: 978-1-84968-150-6   Paperback: 276 pages

Over 45 recipes to take you from beginner to professional in SharePoint Development

1. Learn the most important SharePoint 2010 development skills quickly

2. Progress through a carefully thought out selection of topics that build upon each other as you move through the book.

3. Build "schema" for SharePoint data and leverage that schema appropriately in your application.

Please check **www.PacktPub.com** for information on our titles

www.ingramcontent.com/pod-product-compliance
Lightning Source LLC
La Vergne TN
LVHW062317060326
832902LV00013B/2270